I CAN SAY THE S SOUND!

Speech Therapy Workbook

MEREDITH AVREN, M.ED., CCC-SLP

I CAN SAY THE S SOUND!

I CAN SAY THE S SOUND!
Speech Therapy Workbook
MEREDITH AVREN, M.ED., CCC-SLP

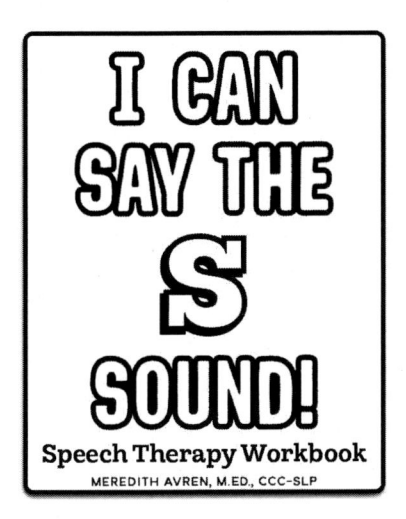

Copyright © 2017, 2018 by Meredith Avren

Written by Meredith Avren, M.Ed., CCC-SLP

All rights reserved. Pages in this book may be reproduced to share with clients and parents for personal use. Otherwise, no part of this book may be reproduced, transmitted, or stored in an information retrieval system in any form or by any means, graphic, electronic, or mechanical, including photocopying, taping and recording, without prior written permission from the publisher. In accordance of the U.S. Copyright Act of 1976, any violation is unlawful piracy and theft of the authors' and illustrator's intellectual property.

If you would like to use material from the book other than for personal or client personal use, prior written permission must be obtained by contacting the publisher at permissions@avrenbooks.com. Thank you for your support of the creators' rights.

I Can Say the S Sound - Second Edition 2018

Library of Congress Catalog Card Number pending

ISBN 978-0-9995964-2-5
10 9 8 7 6 5 4 3 2 1

Published by Avren Books™

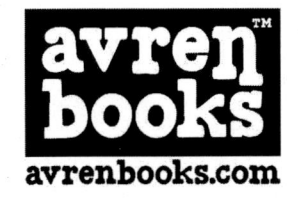

avren books™
avrenbooks.com

TABLE OF CONTENTS

A NOTE FOR THE SPEECH-LANGUAGE PATHOLOGIST FROM THE AUTHOR ... 7
WHY IS THE S SOUND CHALLENGING? ... 8
SPEECH SOUND SELF REPORT ... 9
SPEECH ANATOMY: LEARNING ABOUT THE PARTS OF THE MOUTH ... 10-11
I CAN SAY THE S SOUND POSTER ... 12
VISUALS FOR THE S SOUND ... 13
HOW TO PRODUCE THE S SOUND ... 15-16
COMMON S ERRORS - FRONTAL VS. LATERAL LISP ... 17
PULL BACK METHOD - ELICITING AN S SOUND FROM A TH SOUND ... 18
TOOLS FOR TEACHING THE S SOUND ... 19
UNDERSTANDING AIRFLOW ... 20
JAW STABILITY ... 21-22
STRETCHY T - ELICITING AN S SOUND FROM A T SOUND ... 23
STRETCHY T PRACTICE ... 24-31
FACILITATING CONTEXTS ... 33-36
S PRACTICE - DRILL SHEETS FOR PRACTICE IN ISOLATION ... 37-39
MINIMAL PAIRS CARDS ... 41
S IN SYLLABLES ... 43
SAY AND DOT S PRACTICE ... 44-57
SPIN IT, SAY IT, COLOR IT ... 58-60
CARRIER PHRASE FUN ... 61-63
TALLY SHEET WITH WORD LISTS: PRACTICE AND DATA COLLECTION ... 64-65
ARTICULATION TIC-TAC-TOE ... 66
WORD TO PICTURE MATCHING ... 67-69
S CLUES: CUT AND PASTE ... 71-81
SILLY SENTENCES: READ AND ILLUSTRATE ... 83-89
STORY TIME: READ AND ILLUSTRATE S STORIES ... 90-101
WRITING PAGES ... 102-103
RESOURCES ... 105

ALL RIGHTS RESERVED © 2017 peachiespeechie.com

A NOTE FOR THE SPEECH-LANGUAGE PATHOLOGIST

I hope this workbook helps you as you work with your client to help them achieve accurate production of the S sound.

This workbook is a collection of instructional sheets, practice pages, crafts, and activities that have helped me successfully motivate and teach my students to produce the S sound. This workbook is not a replacement for speech therapy, of course. It is simply a collection of materials that speech-language pathologists may find useful during therapy sessions.

If you have any questions, suggestions, or comments please feel free to email me at meredith@peachiespeechie.com

Meredith Avren, M. Ed., CCC-SLP

Important disclaimer about this resource, "I Can Say the S Sound": This workbook and the techniques presented in it are designed to be used by a speech-language pathologist with an in-depth knowledge of anatomy and speech sound production. Users must use professional judgment and common sense when implementing techniques described in this product. Appropriate techniques vary based on the individual being treated.

WHY IS THE S SOUND CHALLENGING?

The S sound can be challenging to produce, and also challenging for the speech-language pathologist to correct. In the school setting, clinicians often wait to correct the S sound until the child is older, making the error sound a strong habit.

To accurately produce the S sound, the back lateral margins of the tongue are elevated and the blade of the tongue almost touches the alveolar ridge. Air is directed through the midline groove of the tongue and through the constriction between the alveolar ridge and tongue blade. The tip of the tongue can be either up, right behind the top front teeth or down right behind the bottom front teeth.

Tongue position, jaw position, and airflow all have to be just right to produce an accurate S sound.

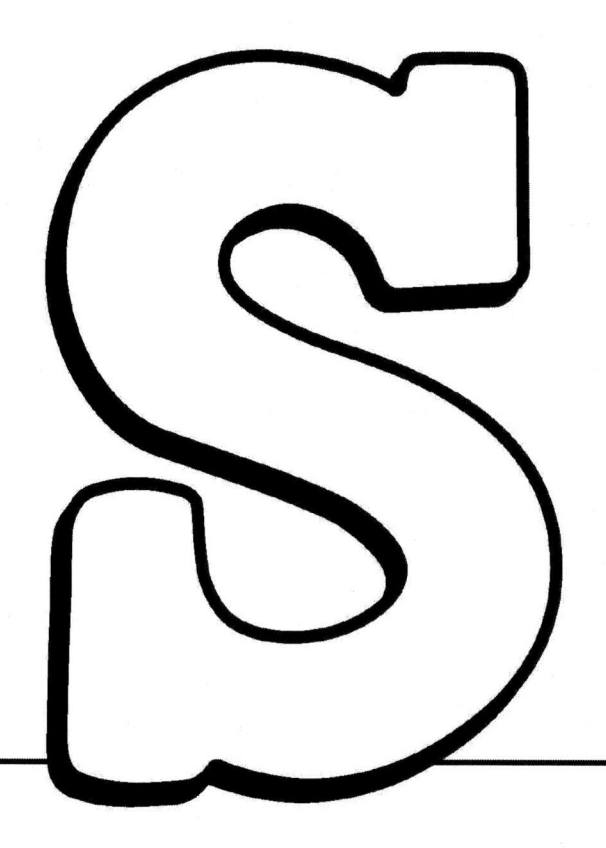

SELF REPORT

How is My Speech?

| Do you have difficulty producing one or more speech sounds? | YES | NO | I DON'T KNOW |

| How do you feel about your speech? | 🙂 | 😐 | ☹️ |

| Do you want to work on improving your speech? | ✓ YES | ✗ NO |

| Do you feel confident when talking to your peers? | YES, ALWAYS | NO, NEVER | SOMETIMES |

| Do other people point out differences in your speech? | YES, ALWAYS | NO, NEVER | SOMETIMES |

| Do you feel frustrated when speaking? | YES, OFTEN | NO, NEVER | SOMETIMES |

What else would you like to tell me about your speech?

ALL RIGHTS RESERVED © 2017 PEACHIESPEECHIE.COM

I CAN SAY THE S SOUND!

Speech Anatomy: Let's learn about parts of the mouth!

Before we start working on specific speech sounds, let's learn about the body parts used in speech production. We will learn about the following structures: lips, tongue (tip and back of the tongue), alveolar ridge, teeth (front teeth and molars), and jaw.

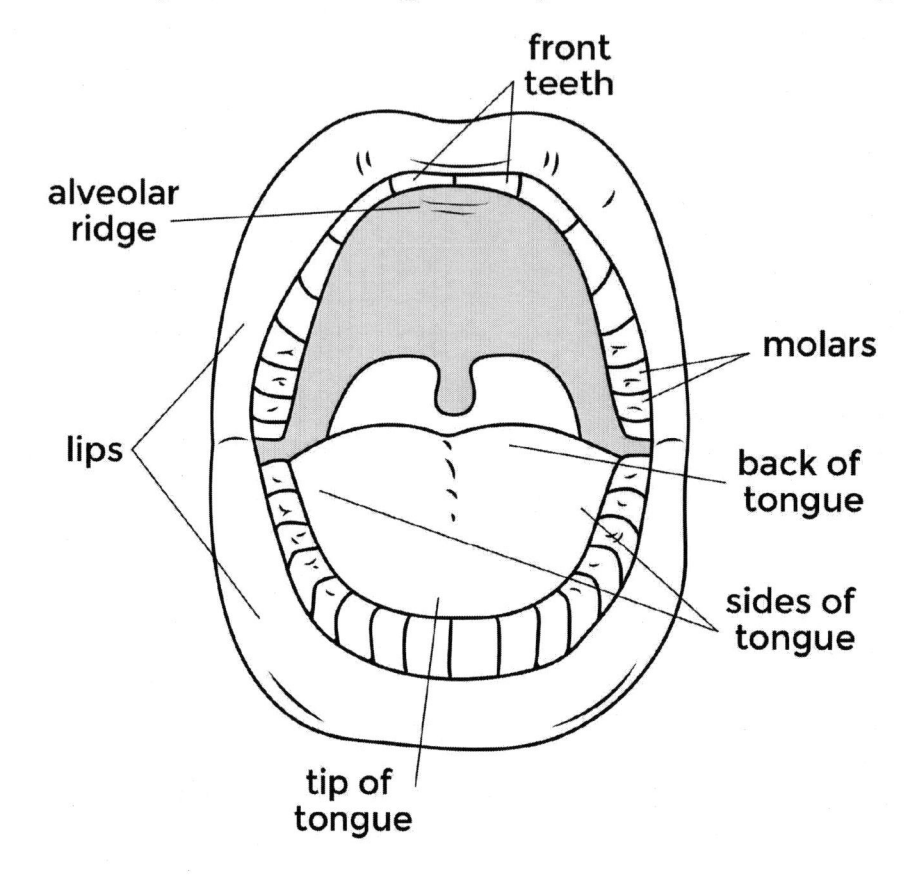

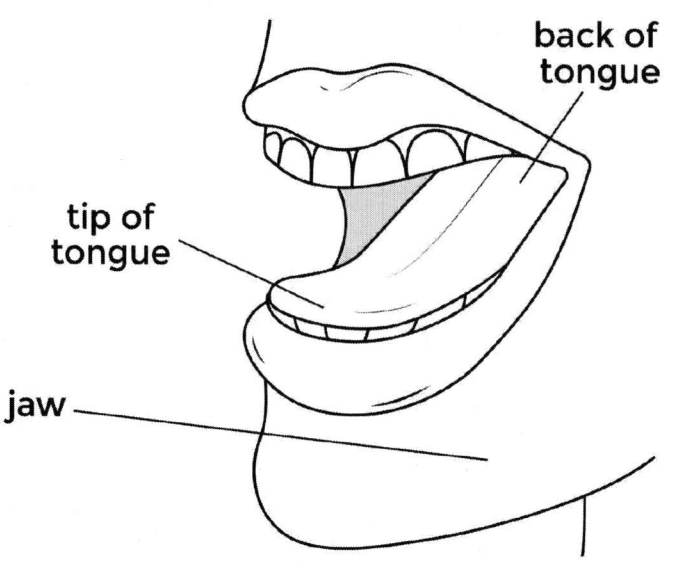

- front teeth
- alveolar ridge
- molars
- back of tongue
- sides of tongue
- lips
- tip of tongue

- back of tongue
- tip of tongue
- jaw

ALL RIGHTS RESERVED © 2017 peachiespeechie.com

I CAN SAY THE S SOUND!

Speech Anatomy: Label the body parts below.

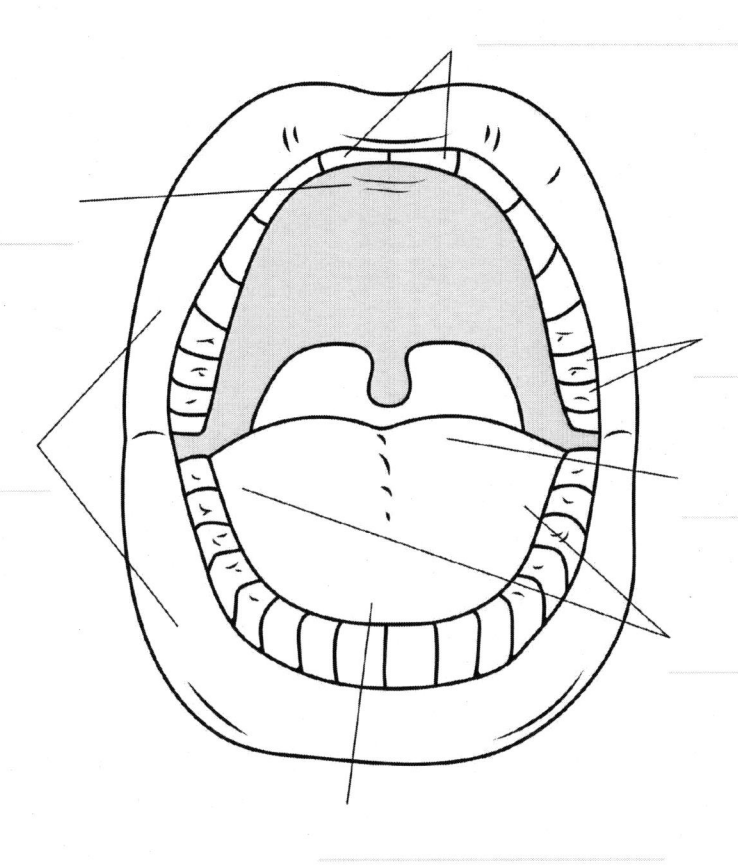

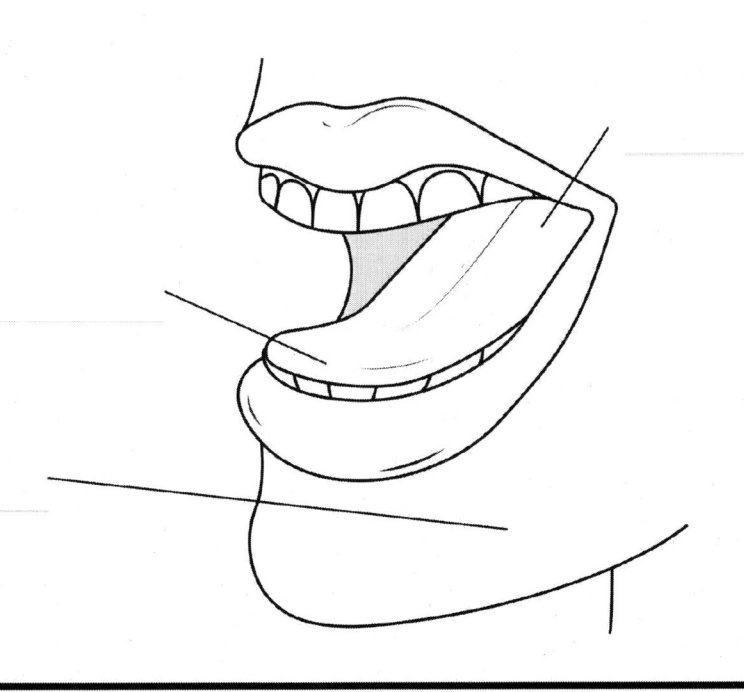

I can say the S sound!

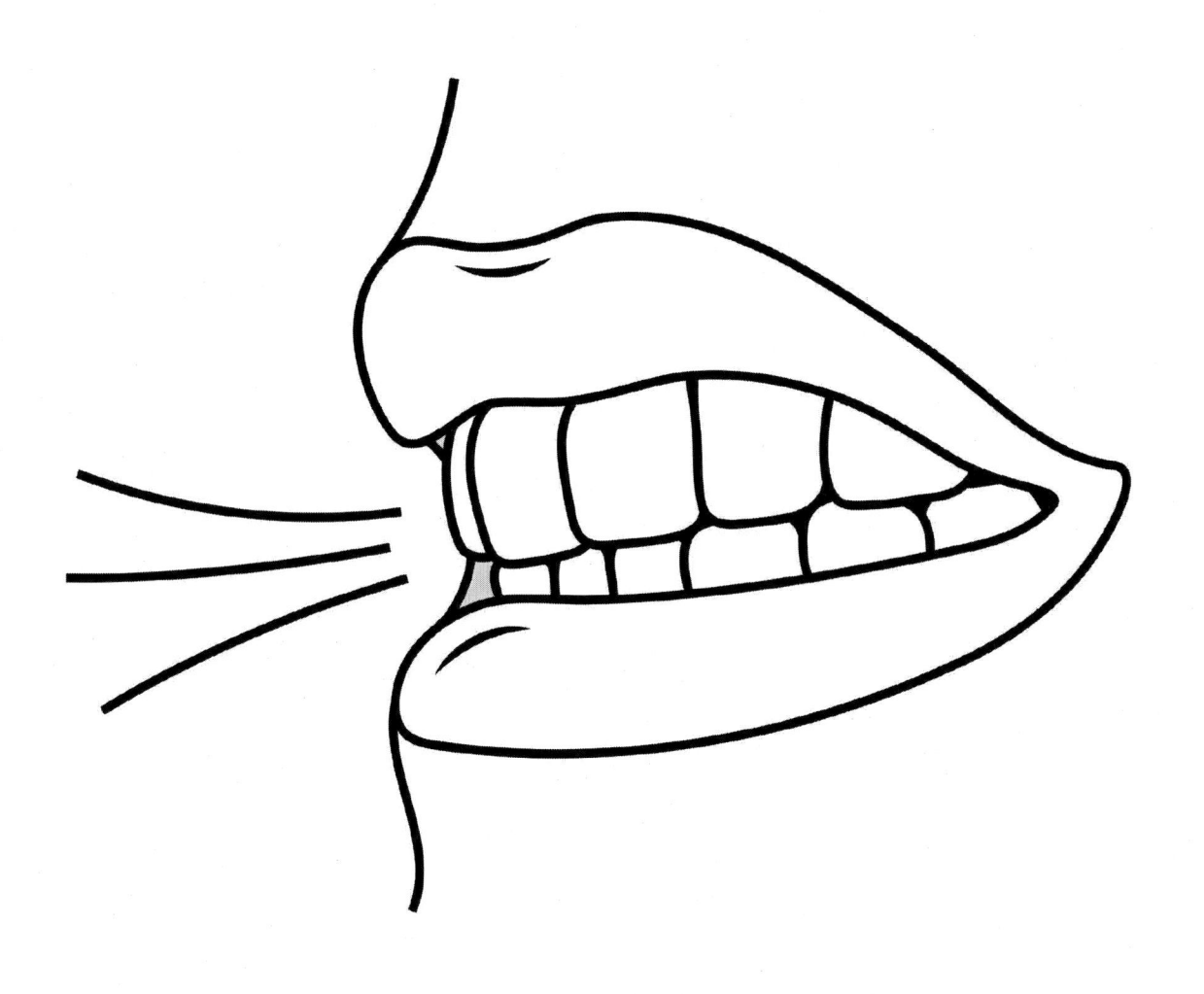

I CAN SAY THE S SOUND!

S Sound Visuals

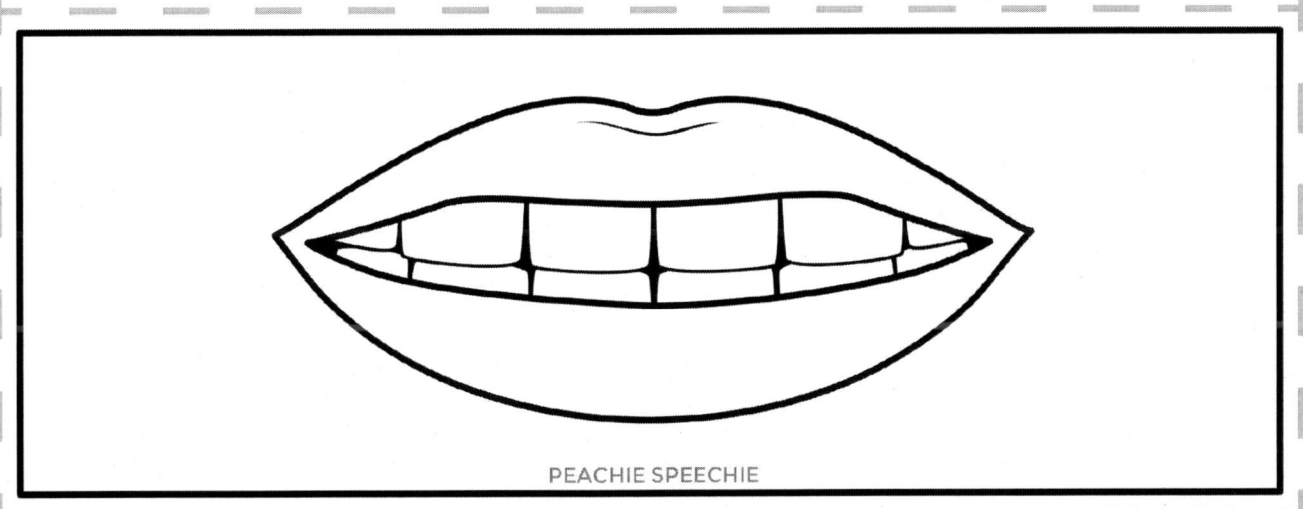

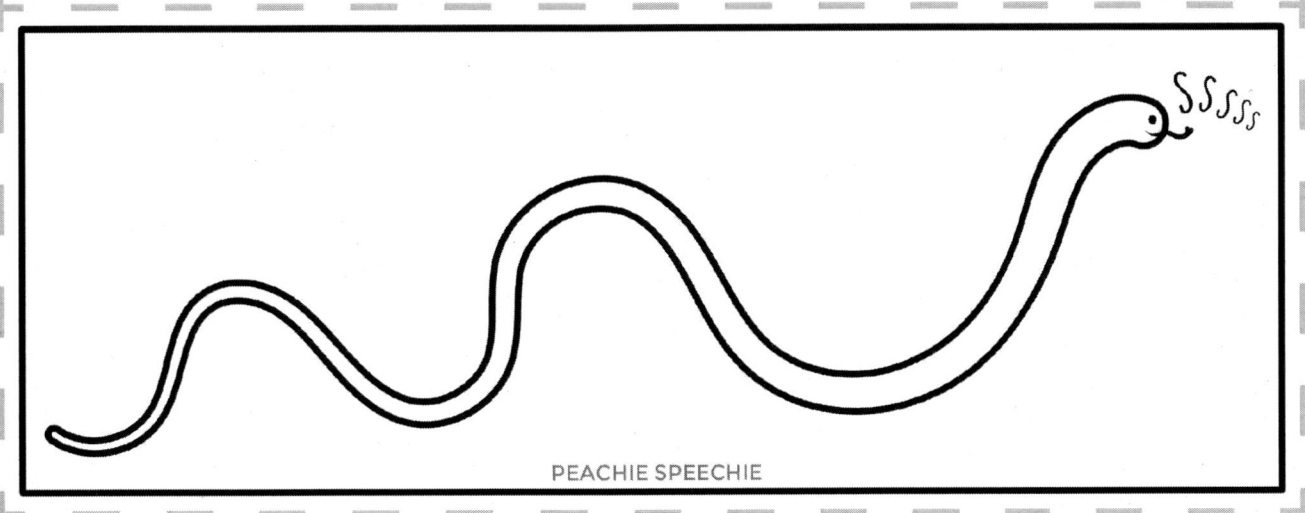

ssssssssssssssssssssss

PEACHIE SPEECHIE

PEACHIE SPEECHIE

SSsss

PEACHIE SPEECHIE

ALL RIGHTS RESERVED © 2017 PEACHIESPEECHIE.COM

HOW TO PRODUCE THE S SOUND

Close your jaw, keeping your tongue behind your teeth. Gently bite your teeth together.

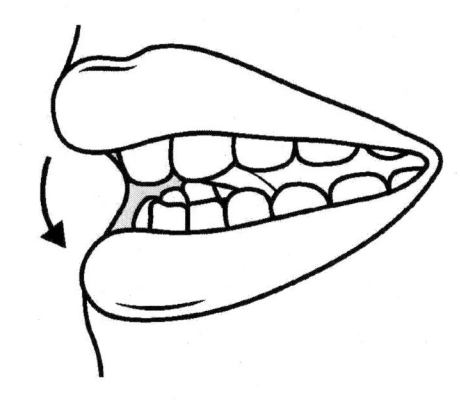

Retract your lips by smiling.

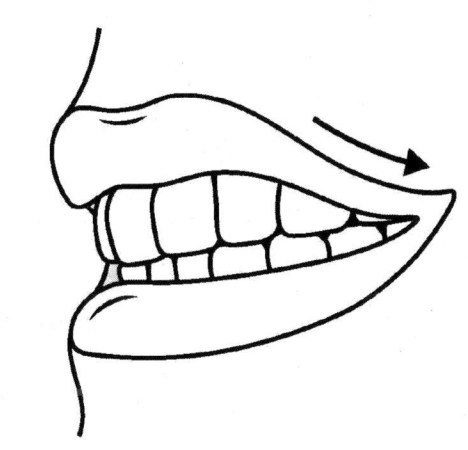

Release air. As you exhale, send air forward over your tongue.

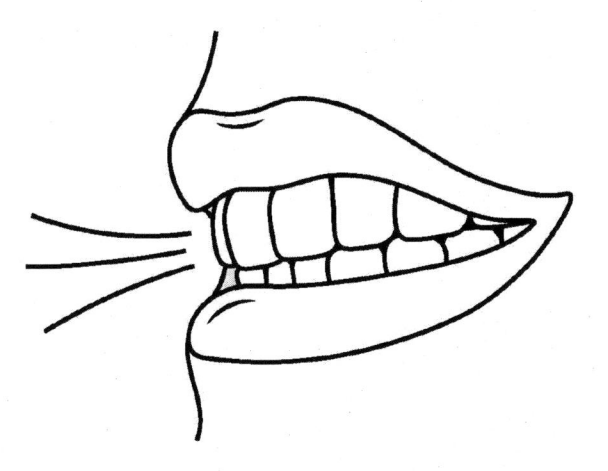

*Note: This technique is designed to help stabilize the jaw while keeping the tongue back behind the teeth. As the client improves their ability to control their mouth movements, they won't need to bite their teeth together, and will be able to produce S without their molars touching.

ALL RIGHTS RESERVED © 2017 PEACHIESPEECHIE.COM

I CAN SAY THE S SOUND!

Tip Down S vs. Tip Up S: Let's learn about two ways to produce the S sound!

When producing the S sound, some people hold their tongue tip up just below the alveolar ridge.

Tip Up S

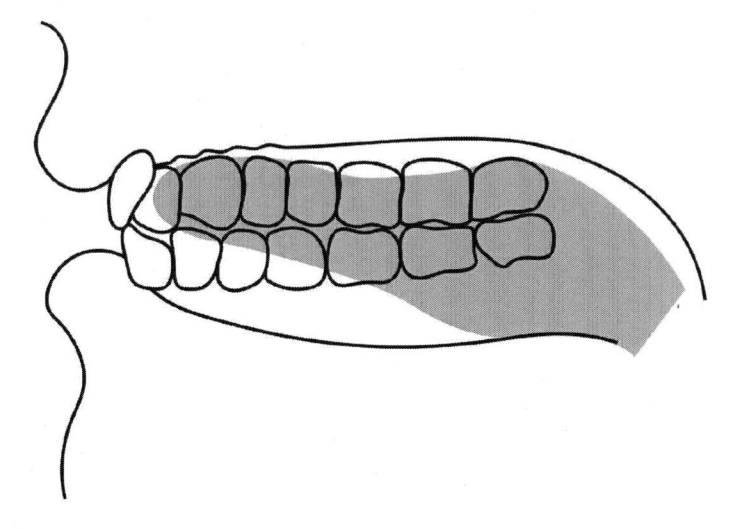

Other people curl their tongue tip down behind the bottom teeth. In both cases, the blade of the tongue is positioned near the alveolar ridge.

Tip Down S

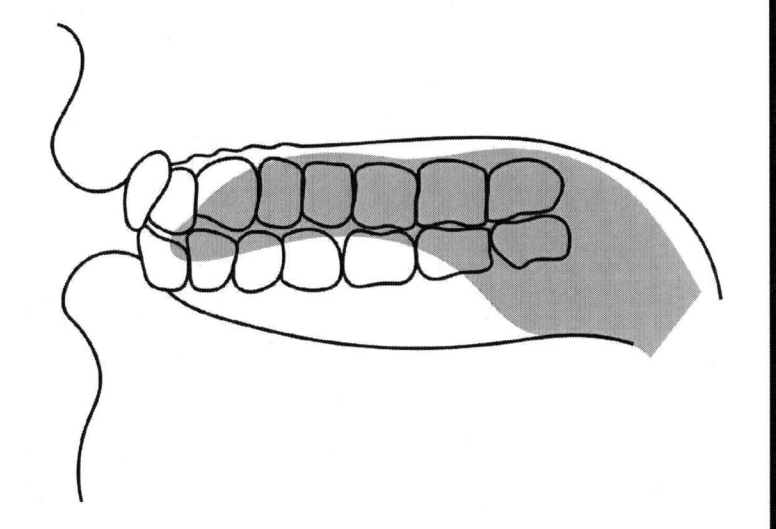

ALL RIGHTS RESERVED © 2017 PEACHIESPEECHIE.COM

I CAN SAY THE S SOUND!

Common S Errors: Frontal vs. Lateral Lisps

Two common errors for the S sound are the frontal lisp and lateral lisp. A frontal lisp occurs when the tongue tip slips through the teeth, and is often heard as the TH sound instead of an S. A lateral lisp occurs when the tongue is improperly positioned and air escapes out of the sides of the mouth, creating a slushy, wet sound instead of a true S sound.

Frontal Lisp

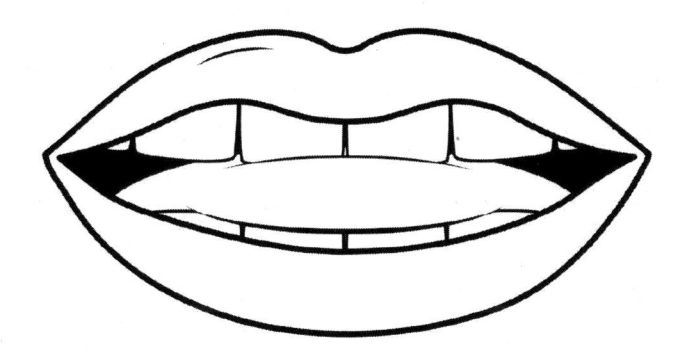

Lateral Lisp

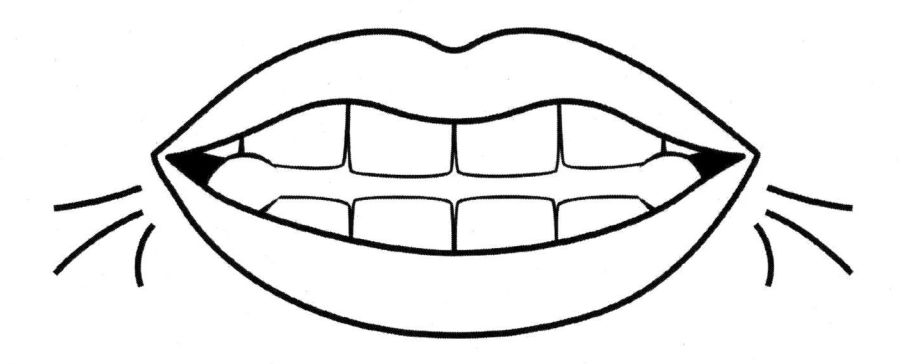

I CAN SAY THE S SOUND!

Pull Back: Moving the tongue from a TH to an S position

Start by producing the TH sound.

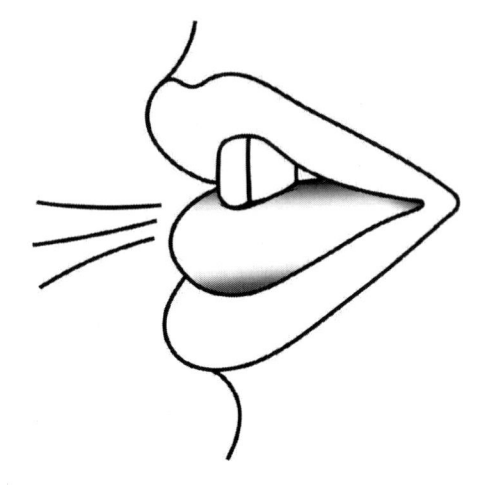

Pull the tongue back behind the teeth while continuing airflow.

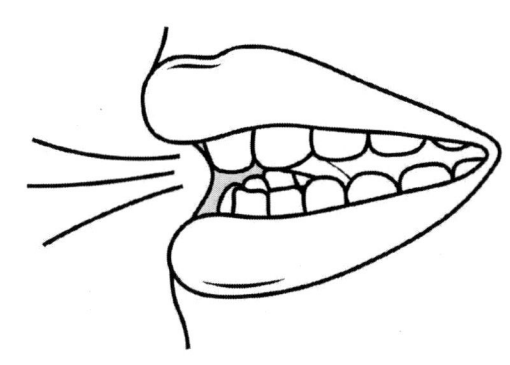

Close jaw slightly once the tongue is behind the teeth.

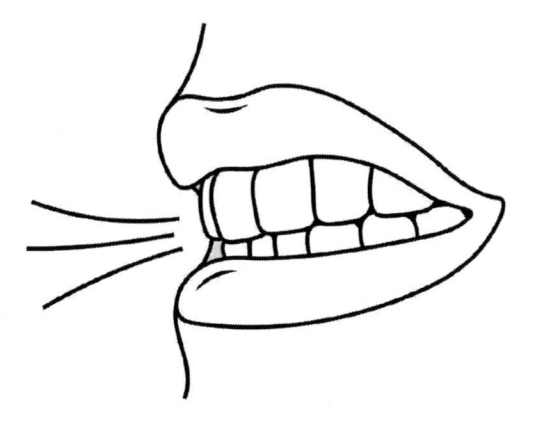

I CAN SAY THE S SOUND!

Tools for Teaching the S Sound

Sometimes verbal placement instructions, models, and illustrations are not enough to teach a child to say the S sound. For these children, additional tactile input can be helpful. The following tools can be used to increase a child's awareness of their oral structures, airflow, and help guide them into the correct oral position. Each child is different, and it is up to their speech-language pathologist to decide which tools are most appropriate during therapy sessions.

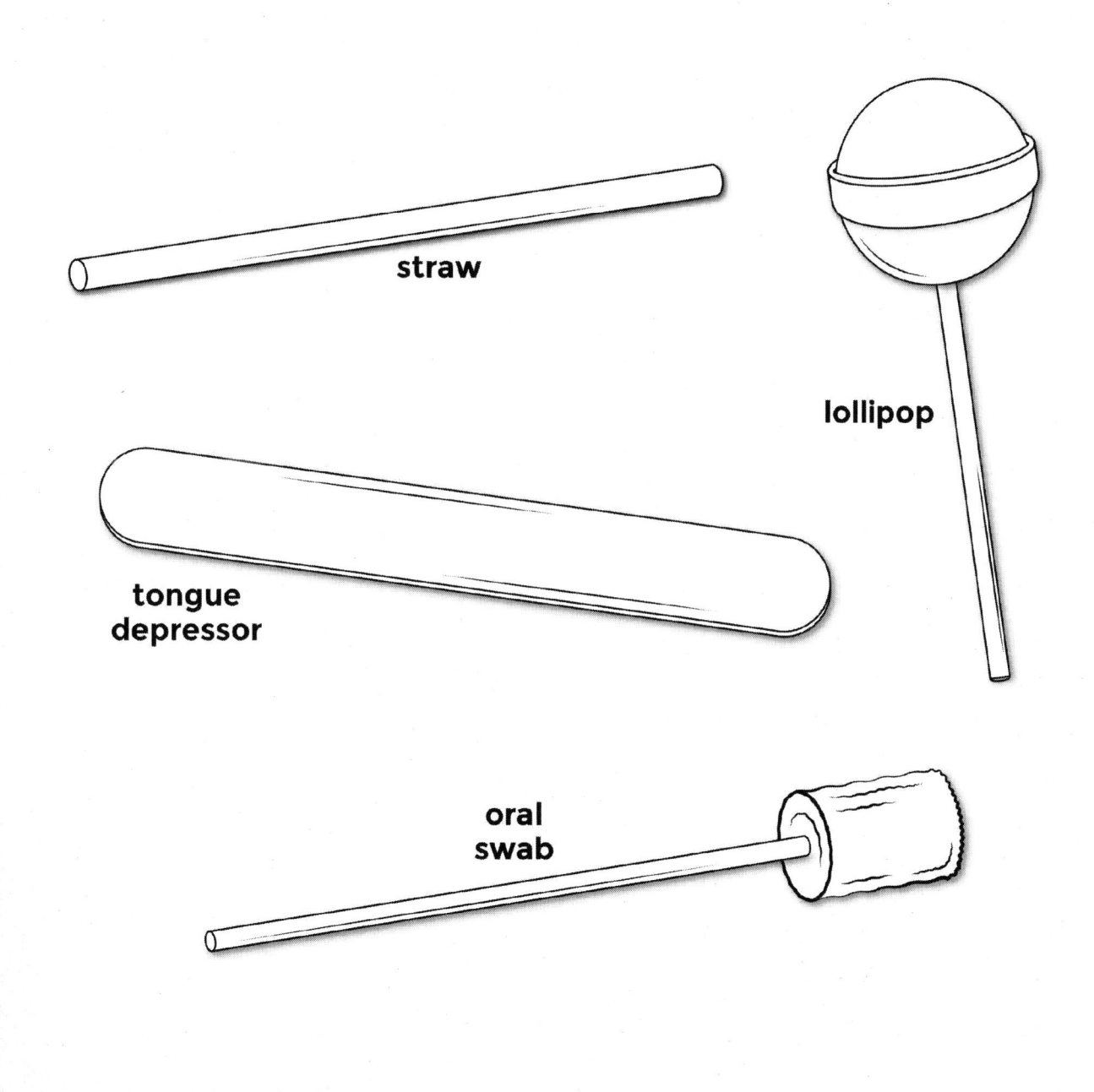

straw

lollipop

tongue depressor

oral swab

I CAN SAY THE S SOUND!

Using a Straw to Understand Airflow

It is important to have a forward midline air stream when producing the S sound. If a child produces a lateralized S, you can increase their awareness of airflow using a straw.

Ask your client to produce the S sound while holding a staw up to their mouth as pictured. If an accurate S is produced with forward airflow, they will hear the air rushing through the straw when it is centered in front of their front teeth. If a lateralized S is produced, air will be heard rushing through the straw when it is held up to the side of the mouth.

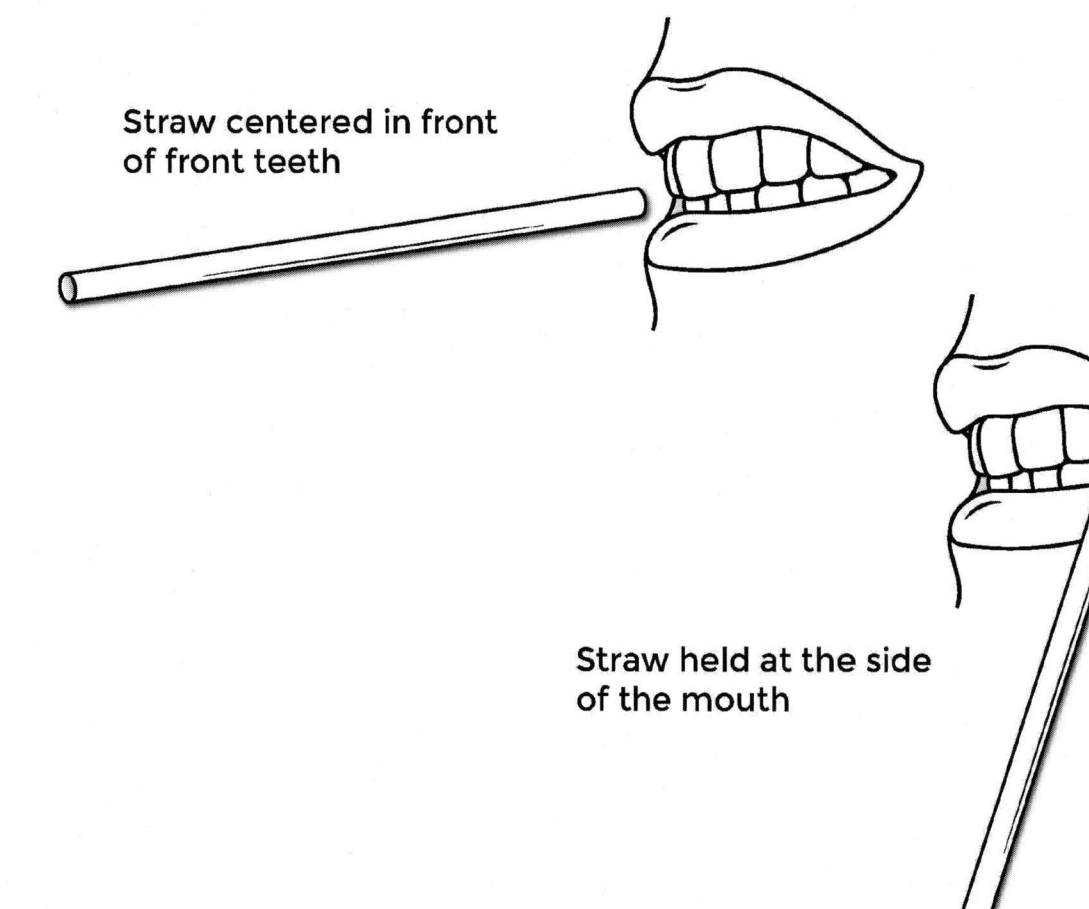

Straw centered in front of front teeth

Straw held at the side of the mouth

ALL RIGHTS RESERVED © 2017 PEACHIESPEECHIE.COM

I CAN SAY THE S SOUND!

Jaw Stability for Production of the S Sound

Jaw instability is often seen in clients with a frontal lisp. When a frontal lisp, or dentalized /s/ sound is produced, the jaw drops too low.

Demonstrate the differences in jaw placement by producing an accurate /s/ sound for your client. Have them touch under your chin while you do this.

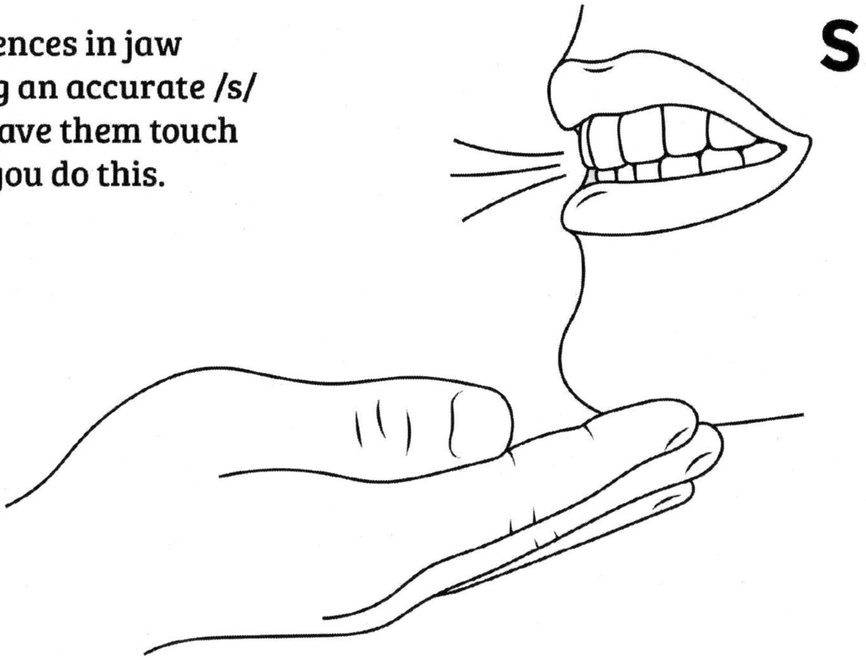

S

Then, with your client still touching your chin, move into production of a dentalized /s/ or TH sound. Your client will be able to feel the lowering of your jaw as you change sounds.

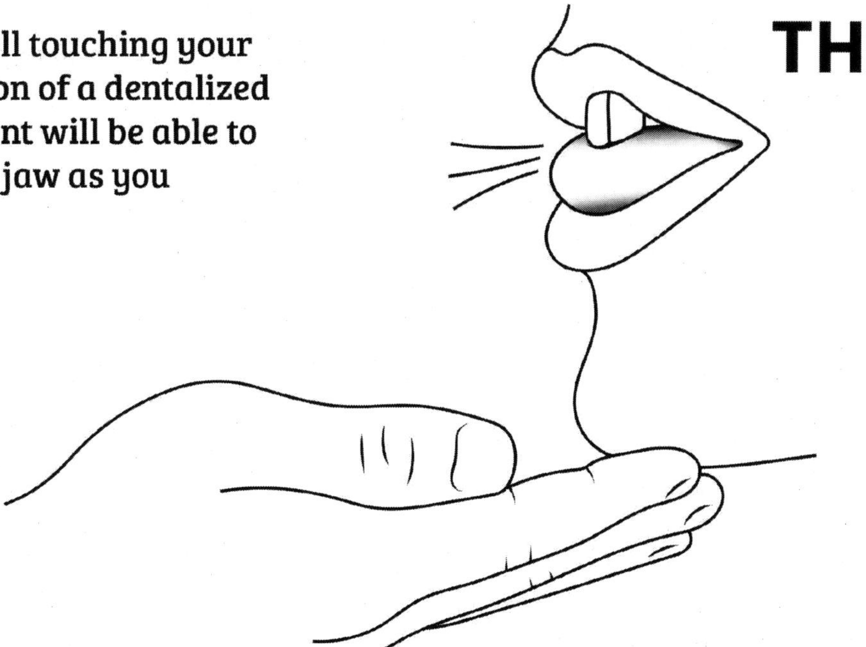

TH

ALL RIGHTS RESERVED © 2017 PEACHIESPEECHIE.COM

I CAN SAY THE S SOUND!

Jaw Stability for Production of the S Sound

To achieve the stability necessary to produce a clear, accurate, S sound, you'll want to teach your client to do 2 things:

- Keep the jaw high
- Keep the back lateral margins of the tongue high, touching the back molars

To help keep the jaw stable during production of the S sound, you can use a small coffee straw. Have the client hold the straw between molars on one side of the mouth as pictured. If their jaw drops out of place, the straw will slide out of place. Instruct them to keep the straw in place while they practice.

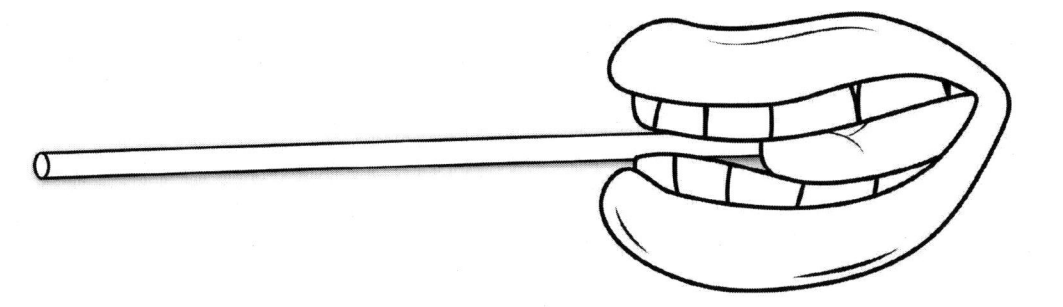

To help increase awareness of the back lateral margins of the tongue, you can swipe it with a sour lollipop. Rub each back lateral margin and tell your client to keep the sides up, touching their back molars.

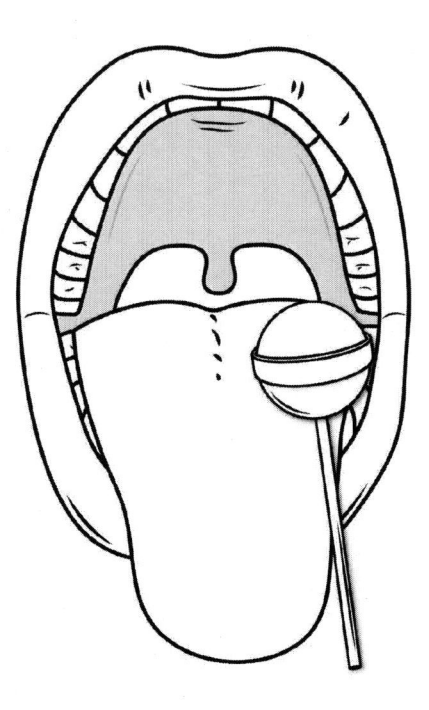

ALL RIGHTS RESERVED © 2017 peachiespeechie.com

I CAN SAY THE S SOUND!

Stretchy T: Eliciting an S-sound from a T-sound

Start with the T sound. Practice saying T by itself, "T-T-T-T".

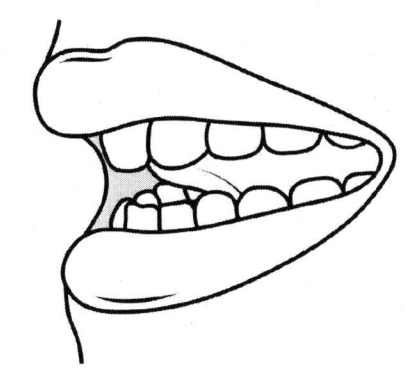

Stretch out the T, making it longer. Do this by adding more air when you say the T sound.

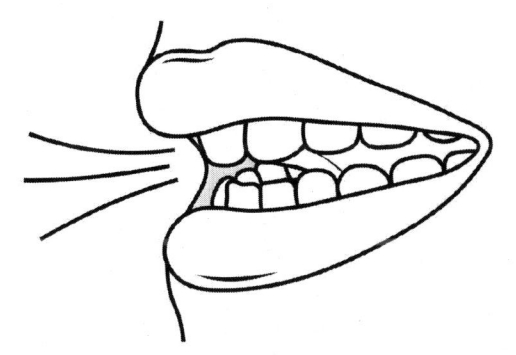

Now, Make the release of air even longer. It will sound like "TSSsssss".

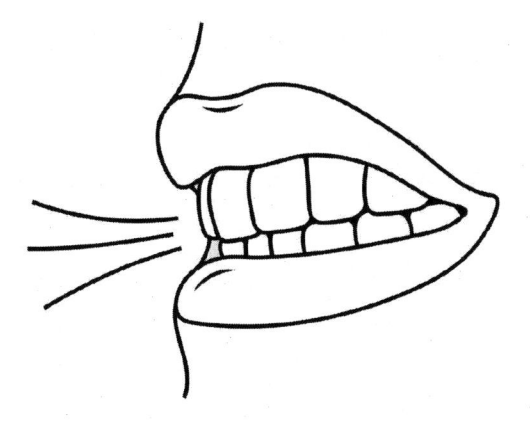

ALL RIGHTS RESERVED © 2017 PEACHIESPEECHIE.COM

I CAN SAY THE S SOUND!

Stretchy T Practice: Eliciting an S-sound from a T-sound

Say the T sound each time you see the Ⓣ. When you see the T⟶, stretch out your T sound. Add more air and make it a long sound. Tap each circled T as you practice.

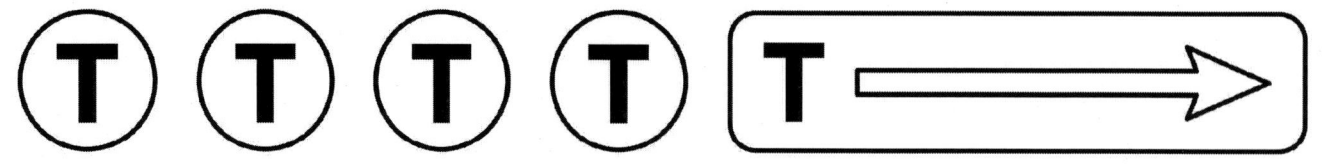

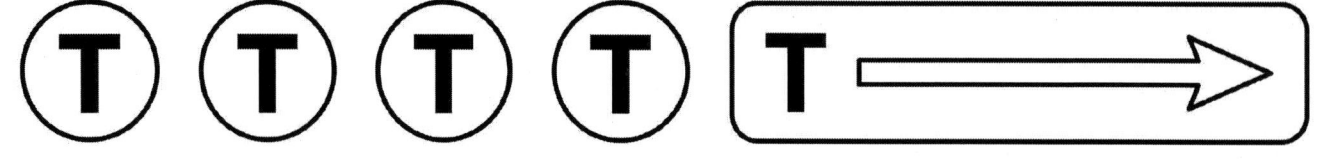

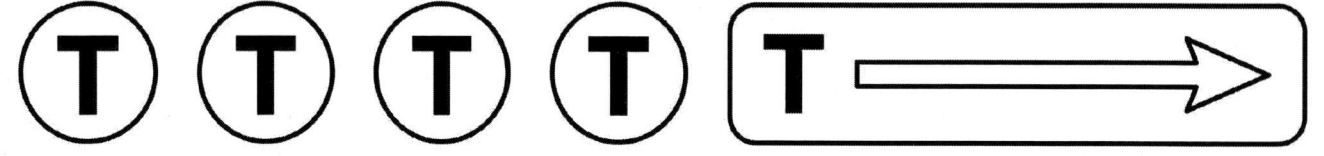

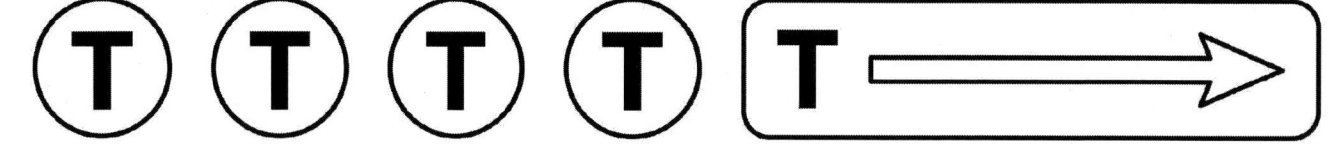

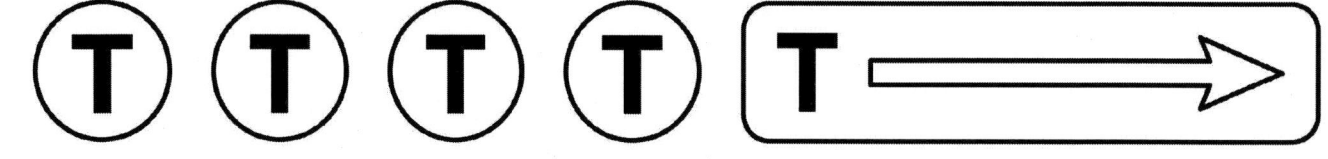

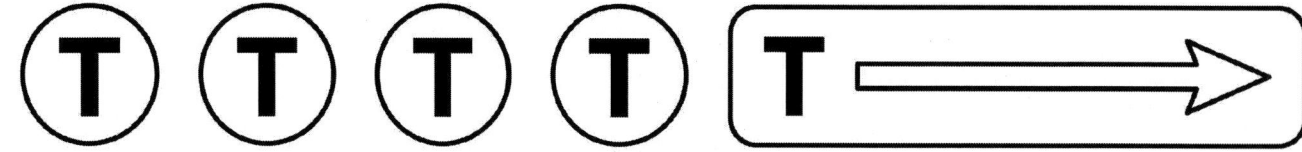

ALL RIGHTS RESERVED © 2017 peachiespeechie.com

I CAN SAY THE S SOUND!

Stretchy T Practice: Eliciting an S-sound from a T-sound

Say the T sound each time you see the Ⓣ. When you see the [TS ⟶], stretch out your T sound. Add more air and make it a long sound. Tap each circled T as you practice.

Ⓣ Ⓣ Ⓣ Ⓣ TS ⟶
Ⓣ Ⓣ Ⓣ Ⓣ TS ⟶
Ⓣ Ⓣ Ⓣ Ⓣ TS ⟶
Ⓣ Ⓣ Ⓣ Ⓣ TS ⟶
Ⓣ Ⓣ Ⓣ Ⓣ TS ⟶
Ⓣ Ⓣ Ⓣ Ⓣ TS ⟶
Ⓣ Ⓣ Ⓣ Ⓣ TS ⟶
Ⓣ Ⓣ Ⓣ Ⓣ TS ⟶
Ⓣ Ⓣ Ⓣ Ⓣ TS ⟶

ALL RIGHTS RESERVED © 2017 PEACHIESPEECHIE.COM

STRETCHY T DRILLS

Practice the words below. Stretch out the last T sound in the word to help you make the **S** sound.

Final TS words

TOTES	GOATS	FLOATS
BOOTS	ROOTS	TOOTS
KITES	LIGHTS	BITES

STRETCHY T DRILLS

Practice the words below. Stretch out the last T sound in the word to help you make the **S** sound.

Final TS words

HITS	BOTS	COTS
TOTS	POTS	DOTS
KNOTS	BOATS	COATS

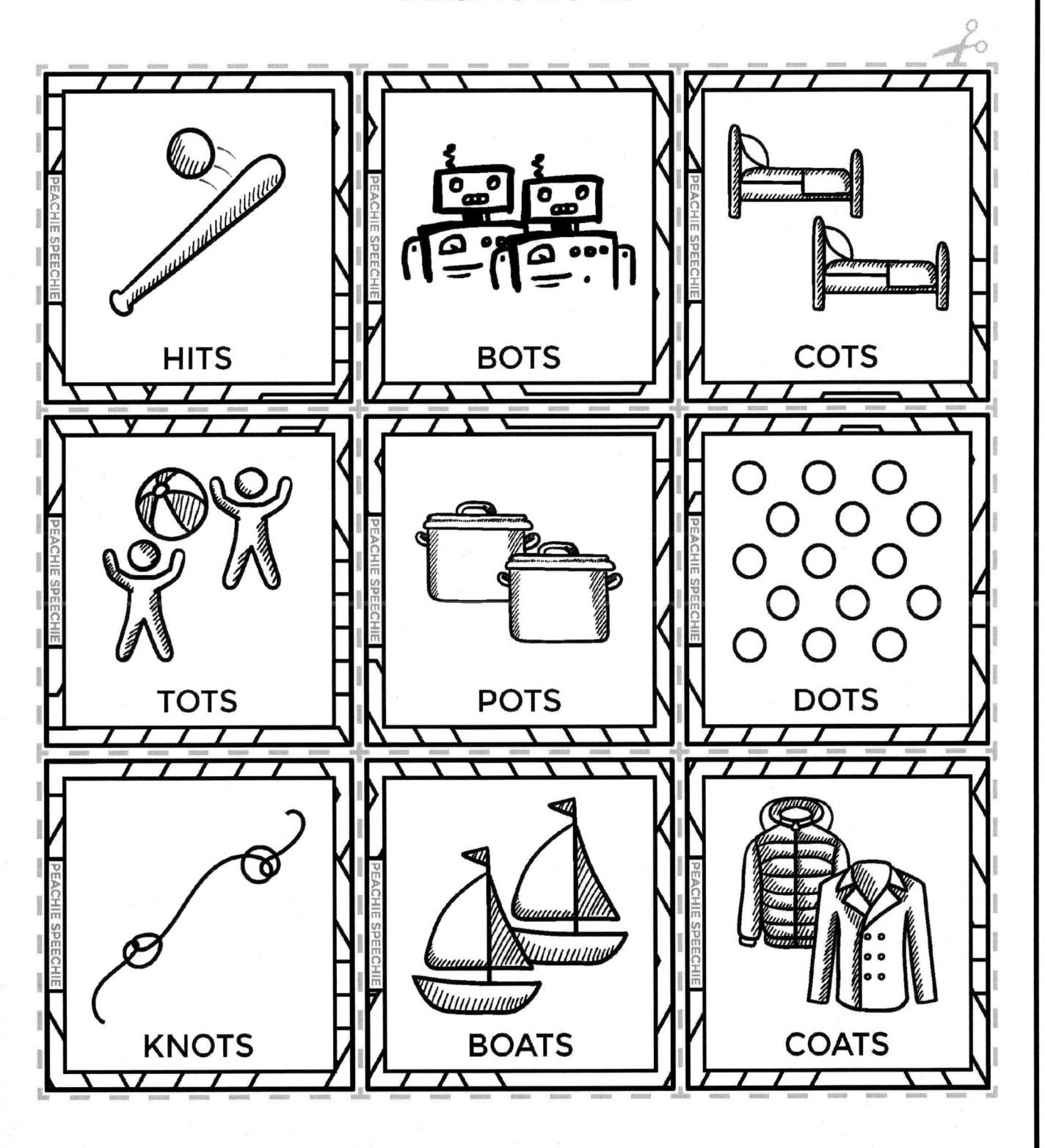

STRETCHY T DRILLS

Practice the words below. Stretch out the last T sound in the word to help you make the **S** sound.

Final TS words

CATS	HATS	MATS
BATS	RATS	GETS
KNITS	"The shoe fits." FITS	PITS

ALL RIGHTS RESERVED © 2017 PEACHIESPEECHIE.COM

I CAN SAY THE S SOUND!

Say each phrase below. As you say the word "hot," stretch out the T sound as you move to the S sound in the following word.

hot _____

- CIDER
- SAND
- SUN
- CELERY
- SANDWICH
- SEAT
- SUMMER
- SODA
- SOUP

Saying 2-word phrases where you transition from a T to an S sound can help with accurate production of S. The T sound is considered a "facilitating context" because it helps you get your tongue positioned for an accurate S sound. (Bernthal, Bankson, & Flipsen, 2009)

ALL RIGHTS RESERVED © 2017 PEACHIESPEECHIE.COM

I CAN SAY THE S SOUND!

Facilitating Contexts for the S Sound

Say each phrase below. As you say the phrase, stretch out the T in the first word to help you say the S in the second word. Say the phrase slowly while holding out the S sound. Say each phrase 5 times, checking a box each time you do it.

HOT SUN ☐ ☐ ☐ ☐ ☐

WET SOCK ☐ ☐ ☐ ☐ ☐

WHITE SAND ☐ ☐ ☐ ☐ ☐

FRUIT SALAD ☐ ☐ ☐ ☐ ☐

EAT SOUP ☐ ☐ ☐ ☐ ☐

I CAN SAY THE S SOUND!

Facilitating Contexts for the S Sound

Say each phrase below. As you say the phrase, stretch out the T in the first word to help you say the S in the second word. Say the phrase slowly while holding out the S sound. Say each phrase 5 times, checking a box each time you do it.

NOT SODA ☐ ☐ ☐ ☐ ☐

WHITE SALT ☐ ☐ ☐ ☐ ☐

FAT SEAL ☐ ☐ ☐ ☐ ☐

BITE SANDWICH ☐ ☐ ☐ ☐ ☐

BOAT SAIL ☐ ☐ ☐ ☐ ☐

ALL RIGHTS RESERVED © 2017 PEACHIESPEECHIE.COM

I CAN SAY THE S SOUND!

These silly phrases will help you stretch out the T sound and turn it into an S sound! Say the word "wet" in the middle and stretch out the final T as you move into saying the S words around it.

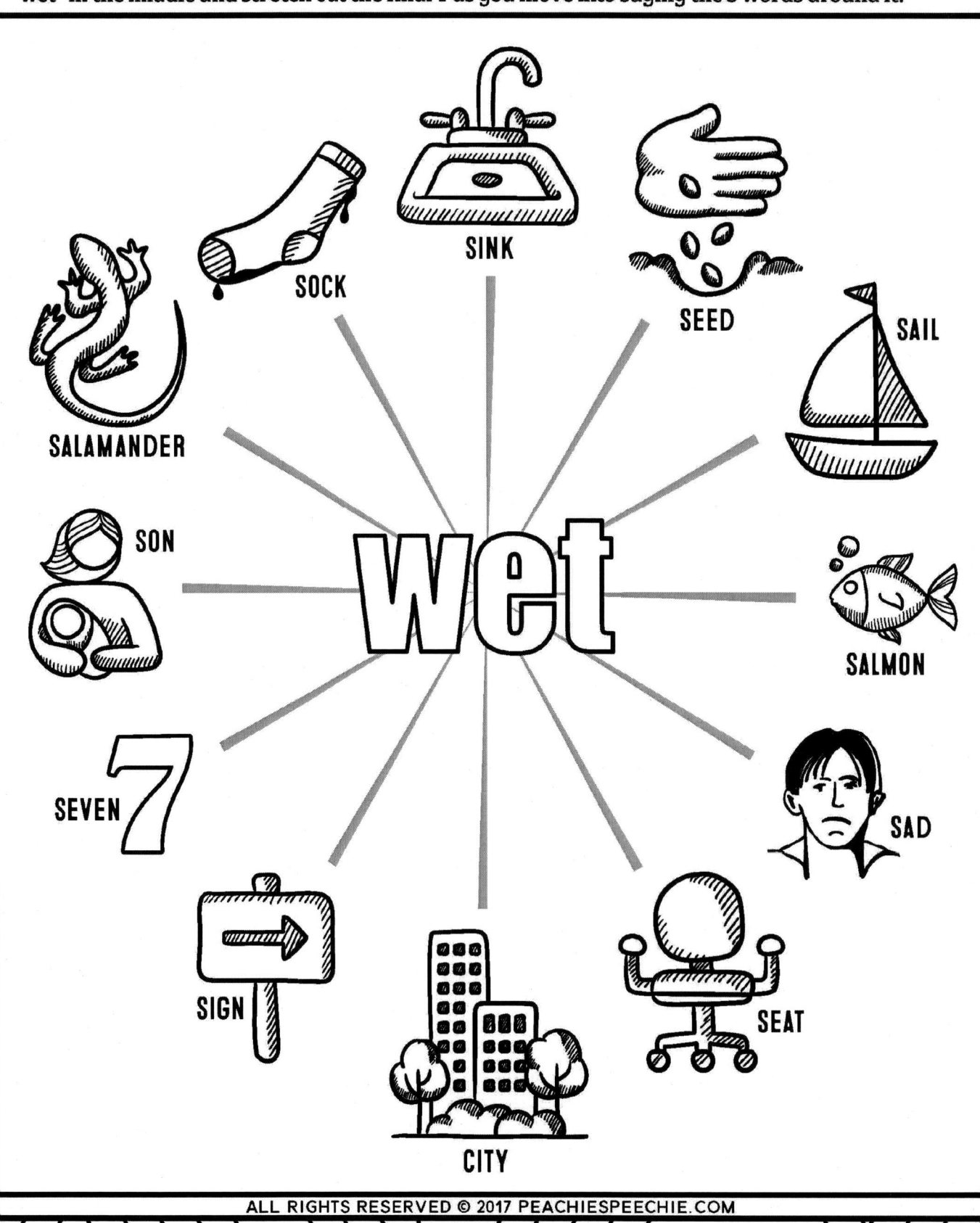

SOCK

SINK

SEED

SAIL

SALAMANDER

SON

wet

SALMON

SEVEN

SAD

SIGN

CITY

SEAT

ALL RIGHTS RESERVED © 2017 peachiespeechie.com

S DRILL PRACTICE

Now that you know how to position your tongue to say the S sound, let's practice! Practice getting your tongue into the correct position and producing the S sound. (Tip: Use a mirror to help if needed!) Color one of the letters below each time you practice.

SUN CHALLENGE

Try to say your S sound 100 times! For every accurate production, color 1 sun.

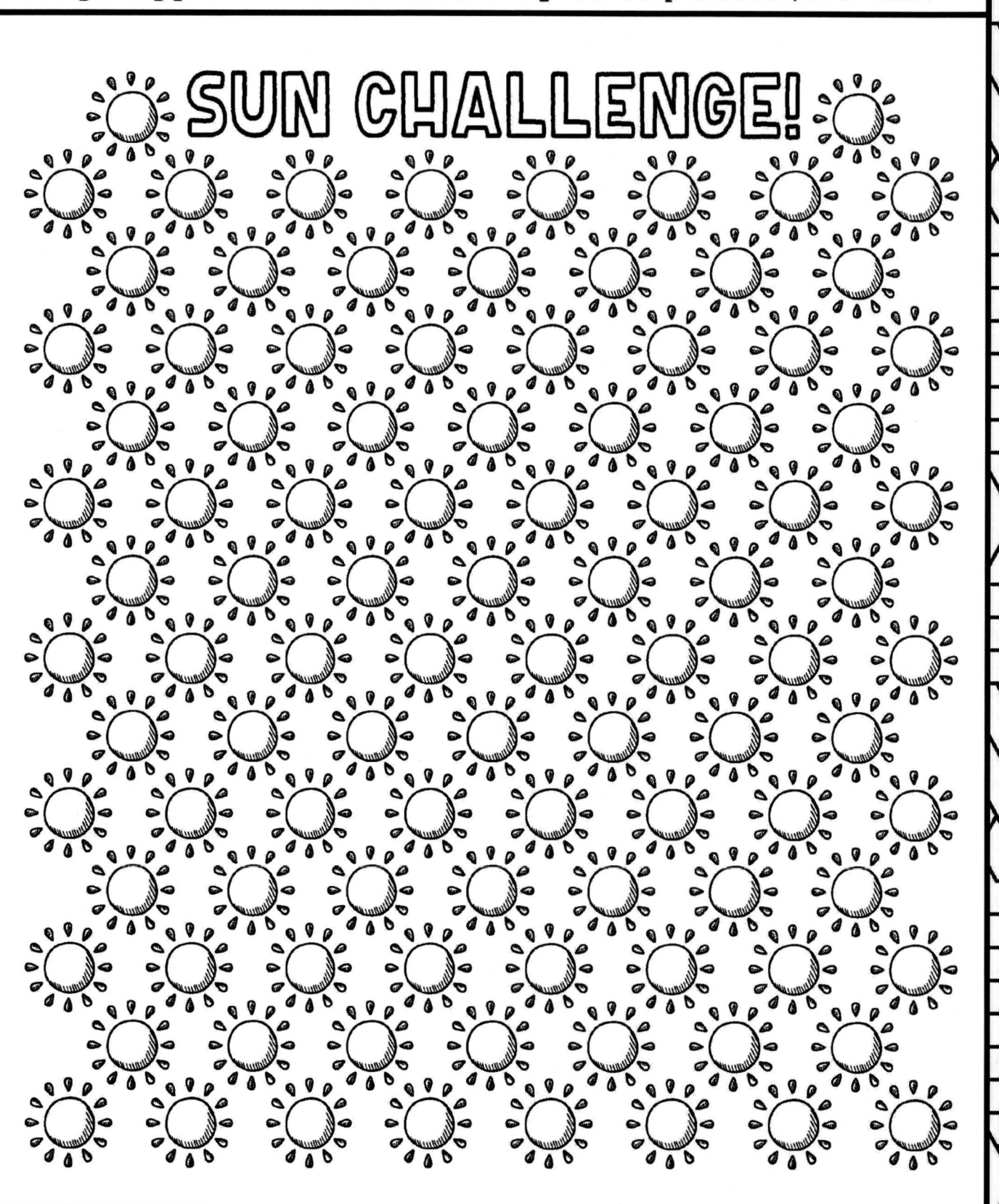

SUN CHALLENGE!

ALL RIGHTS RESERVED © 2017 peachiespeechie.com

S STREET

Use your finger (or a small car or other toy/object) to trace along the road. Every time you get to a sign, stop and practice your sound 5 times.

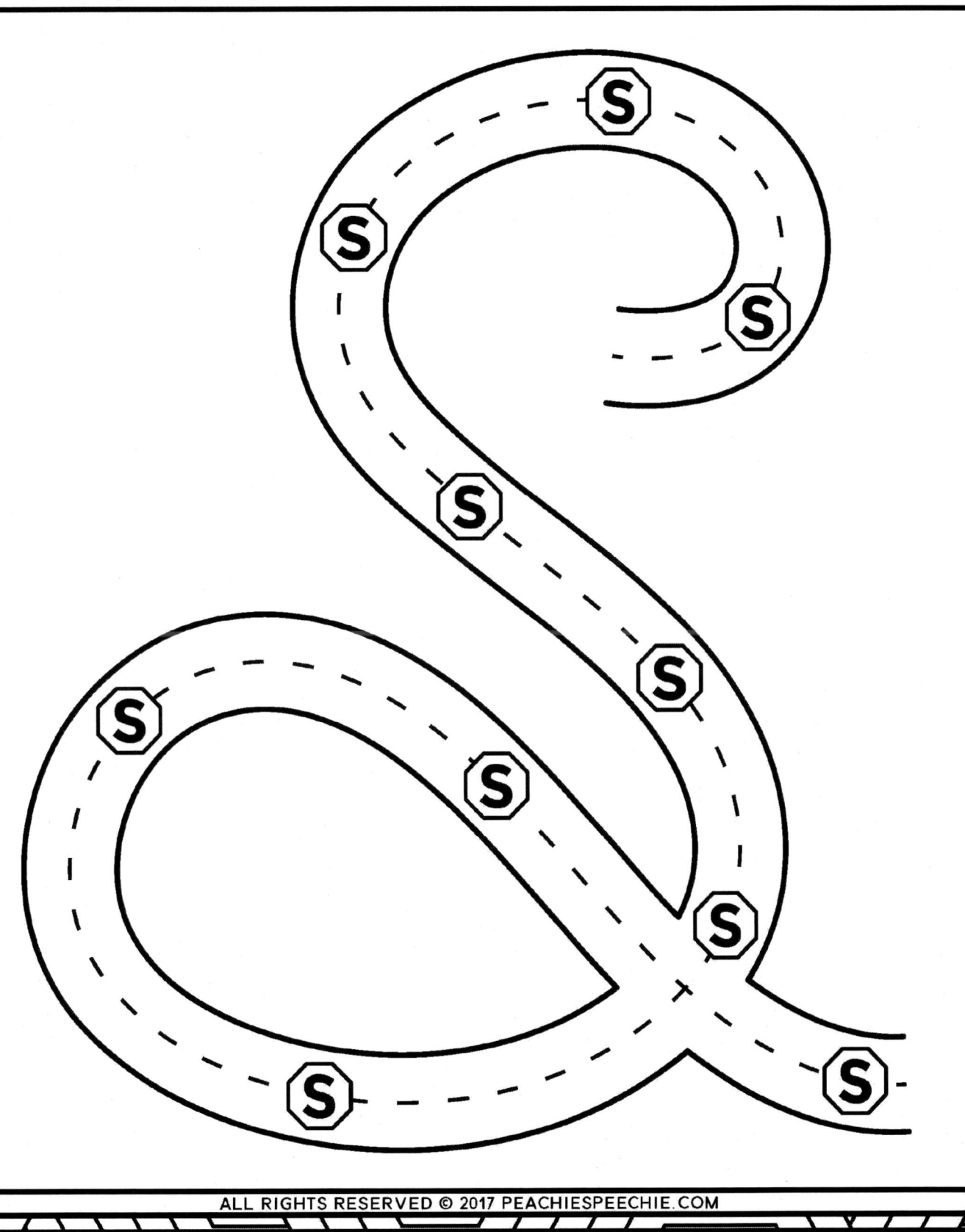

I CAN SAY THE S SOUND!

Minimal Pairs

Listen as your SLP/helper reads the sets of words below. Can you hear the difference between the S sound and the TH sound? Point to the picture of the words you hear. Then, cut out the cards and practice saying the words yourself!

THIGH / SIGH	THINK / SINK	CYMBAL / THIMBLE
THANK / SANK	THAD / SAD	THUMB / SUM
THICK / SICK	THING / SING	THAW / SAW

ALL RIGHTS RESERVED © 2017 PEACHIESPEECHIE.COM

I CAN SAY THE S SOUND!

S

→ a — Say — I say my name.

→ e — See — I see lots of things.

→ i — Sigh — I sigh sometimes.

→ o — Sew — I sew my clothes.

→ u — Sue — My name is Sue.

I CAN SAY THE S SOUND!

Say and Dot: Initial S Words

Mark the circles below as you practice the S sound in words.

Say	See	Sigh	Sew	Sue

You did it! *You did it!* *You did it!* *You did it!* *You did it!*

ALL RIGHTS RESERVED © 2017 PEACHIESPEECHIE.COM

I CAN SAY THE S SOUND!

Say and Dot: Initial S Words

Mark the circles below as you practice the S sound in words.

Sock	Sun	Sack	Sip	Sand

You did it! You did it! You did it! You did it! You did it!

ALL RIGHTS RESERVED © 2017 PEACHIESPEECHIE.COM

I CAN SAY THE S SOUND!

Say and Dot: Initial S Words

Mark the circles below as you practice the S sound in words.

Sandal	Soccer	Surf	Soda	Sing

You did it!   *You did it!*   *You did it!*   *You did it!*   *You did it!*

ALL RIGHTS RESERVED © 2017 peachiespeechie.com

I CAN SAY THE S SOUND!

Say and Dot: Initial S Words

Mark the circles below as you practice the S sound in words.

Salad	Sushi	Saw	Silverware	Solar Panel

You did it! | You did it! | You did it! | You did it! | You did it!

ALL RIGHTS RESERVED © 2017 PEACHIESPEECHIE.COM

I CAN SAY THE S SOUND!

Say and Dot: Initial S Words

Mark the circles below as you practice the S sound in words.

Search	Sippy Cup	Signal	Submarine	Sale

You did it! | You did it! | You did it! | You did it! | You did it!

ALL RIGHTS RESERVED © 2017 peachiespeechie.com

I CAN SAY THE S SOUND!

Say and Dot: Initial S Sound Words That Start With C

Mark the circles below as you practice the S sound in words.

City	Cent	Celebrate	Circle	Cement Truck

You did it! · You did it! · You did it! · You did it! · You did it!

ALL RIGHTS RESERVED © 2017 PEACHIESPEECHIE.COM

I CAN SAY THE S SOUND!

Say and Dot: Initial S-Blend Words

Mark the circles below as you practice the S sound in words.

Snowman	Spill	Student	Snail	Strawberry

You did it! — You did it! — You did it! — You did it! — You did it!

I CAN SAY THE S SOUND!

Say and Dot: Medial S Words

Mark the circles below as you practice the S sound in words.

Fasten	Tossing	Faucet	Castle	Popsicle

You did it! *You did it!* *You did it!* *You did it!* *You did it!*

ALL RIGHTS RESERVED © 2017 PEACHIESPEECHIE.COM

I CAN SAY THE S SOUND!

Say and Dot: Medial S Words

Mark the circles below as you practice the S sound in words.

Medicine	Ice Cream	Message	Dresser	Whistle

You did it! | You did it! | You did it! | You did it! | You did it!

I CAN SAY THE S SOUND!

Say and Dot: Medial S Words

Mark the circles below as you practice the S sound in words.

Baseball	Messy	Bicycle	Crosswalk	Unicycle

You did it! | You did it! | You did it! | You did it! | You did it!

ALL RIGHTS RESERVED © 2017 PEACHIESPEECHIE.COM

I CAN SAY THE S SOUND!

Say and Dot: Medial S Words

Mark the circles below as you practice the S sound in words.

Croissant	Dinosaur	Motorcycle	Braces	Cassette
○	○	○	○	○
○	○	○	○	○
○	○	○	○	○
○	○	○	○	○
○	○	○	○	○
○	○	○	○	○
○	○	○	○	○
You did it!	You did it!	You did it!	You did it!	You did it!

ALL RIGHTS RESERVED © 2017 peachiespeechie.com

I CAN SAY THE S SOUND!

Say and Dot: Final S Words

Mark the circles below as you practice the S sound in words.

Bricks	Mouse	Ice	Dance	Bus

You did it!   *You did it!*   *You did it!*   *You did it!*   *You did it!*

ALL RIGHTS RESERVED © 2017 PEACHIESPEECHIE.COM

I CAN SAY THE S SOUND!

Say and Dot: Final S Words

Mark the circles below as you practice the S sound in words.

Moose	Race	Goose	Horse	Tennis

You did it! | **You did it!** | **You did it!** | **You did it!** | **You did it!**

ALL RIGHTS RESERVED © 2017 peachiespeechie.com

I CAN SAY THE S SOUND!

Say and Dot: Final S Words

Mark the circles below as you practice the S sound in words.

House	Necklace	Police	Purse	Dice

You did it! | You did it! | You did it! | You did it! | You did it!

ALL RIGHTS RESERVED © 2017 peachiespeechie.com

SPIN IT, SAY IT, COLOR IT

Put a paperclip in the middle of the spinner circle. Then, stick the tip of a pencil through one end of the paperclip to form a "spinner." Spin the paperclip and whatever number it lands on is how many times you must practice one of the S words pictured on the page. Select the word you want to practice, say it the correct amount of times, and then color the picture. Do this until all of the pictures are colored.

INITIAL S

- SAVE
- SUBMARINE
- SALT
- CIDER
- SOUP
- SAND
- SADDLE
- SUITCASE
- SUPPER

ALL RIGHTS RESERVED © 2017 peachiespeechie.com

SPIN IT, SAY IT, COLOR IT

Put a paperclip in the middle of the spinner circle. Then, stick the tip of a pencil through one end of the paperclip to form a "spinner." Spin the paperclip and whatever number it lands on is how many times you must practice one of the S words pictured on the page. Select the word you want to practice, say it the correct amount of times, and then color the picture. Do this until all of the pictures are colored.

MEDIAL S

- POPSICLE
- INSECT
- FAUCET
- BICYCLE
- OUTSIDE
- MEDICINE
- DINOSAUR
- BRACES
- CASTLE

ALL RIGHTS RESERVED © 2017 peachiespeechie.com

SPIN IT, SAY IT, COLOR IT

Put a paperclip in the middle of the spinner circle. Then, stick the tip of a pencil through one end of the paperclip to form a "spinner." Spin the paperclip and whatever number it lands on is how many times you must practice one of the S words pictured on the page. Select the word you want to practice, say it the correct amount of times, and then color the picture. Do this until all of the pictures are colored.

FINAL S

- NECKLACE
- GLASS
- POLICE
- CHESS
- PEACE
- FLEECE
- ICE
- BUS
- MOUSE

ALL RIGHTS RESERVED © 2017 peachiespeechie.com

CARRIER PHRASE FUN! — INITIAL S

Say the phrase "I see a _____" along with the S words listed. Remember to move your tongue into the correct position when you say the S sound.

I see a _____.

- SALAD
- SODA
- SWEET POTATO
- SOCCER BALL
- SANDWICH
- SANDAL
- SIGNAL
- SIGN
- SUBMARINE
- SAIL

ALL RIGHTS RESERVED © 2017 peachiespeechie.com

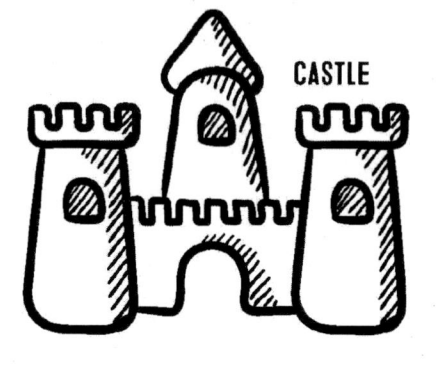

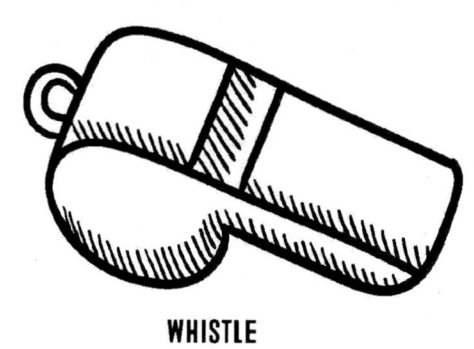

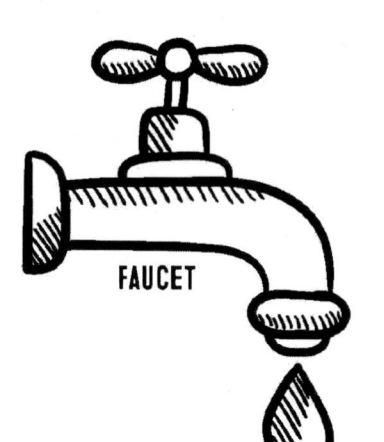

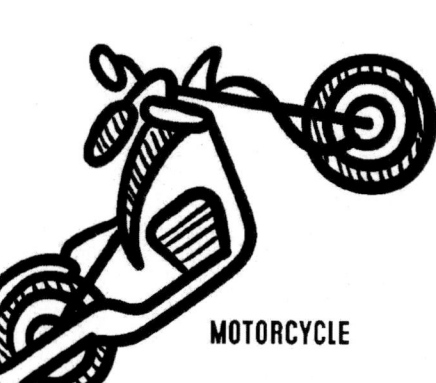

CARRIER PHRASE FUN! — MEDIAL S

Say the phrase "I see a _____" along with the S words listed. Remember to move your tongue into the correct position when you say the S sound.

I see a _____.

- CASTLE
- WHISTLE
- MESSAGE
- FAUCET
- CAROUSEL
- MOTORCYCLE
- BICYCLE
- DANCER
- BASEBALL
- CROISSANT

ALL RIGHTS RESERVED © 2017 PEACHIESPEECHIE.COM

CARRIER PHRASE FUN!

FINAL S

Say the phrase "I see a _____" along with the S words listed. Remember to move your tongue into the correct position when you say the S sound.

I see a _____.

AMBULANCE

FACE

BUS

THERMOS

DRESS

MOOSE

FENCE

RACE

MOUSE

LIGHTHOUSE

ALL RIGHTS RESERVED © 2017 PEACHIESPEECHIE.COM

I CAN SAY THE S SOUND!

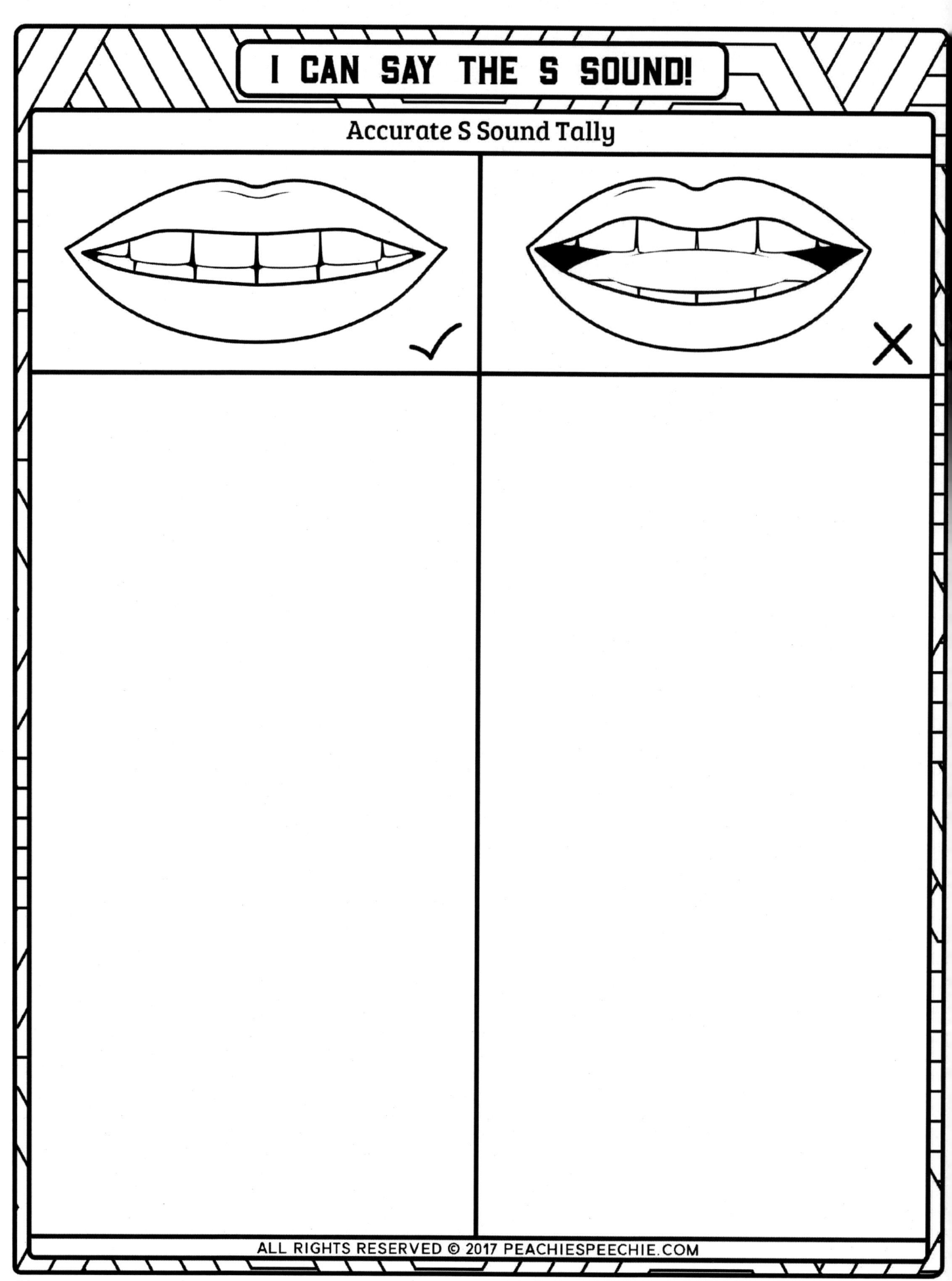

Accurate S Sound Tally

✓	✗

ALL RIGHTS RESERVED © 2017 PEACHIESPEECHIE.COM

S WORD LISTS

Use these words with the tally sheet to mark correct and incorrect productions of the S sound on the tally page.

INITIAL	MEDIAL	FINAL
1. say	1. pencil	1. us
2. saw	2. answer	2. ice
3. same	3. myself	3. nice
4. seem	4. messy	4. mice
5. seed	5. bouncing	5. mouse
6. sea	6. inside	6. house
7. seat	7. outside	7. miss
8. side	8. useful	8. kiss
9. sigh	9. bicycle	9. goose
10. soap	10. whistle	10. geese
11. suit	11. dancing	11. this
12. soup	12. crossing	12. piece
13. soon	13. yesterday	13. place
14. sad	14. message	14. grass
15. sand	15. policeman	15. face
16. sang	16. nicely	16. bus
17. sell	17. possible	17. yes
18. sent	18. tossing	18. horse
19. sing	19. missing	19. guess
20. sunny	20. aside	20. pass

ALL RIGHTS RESERVED © 2017 PEACHIESPEECHIE.COM

I CAN SAY THE S SOUND!

Play tic-tac-toe, but before you take your turn, say the S-word in the square you plan to mark.

ARTICULATION TIC-TAC-TOE!

INITIAL S

SEW	SING	SUN
SODA	SAW	SEED
SOCCER	SILVERWARE	SURFBOARD

INITIAL S

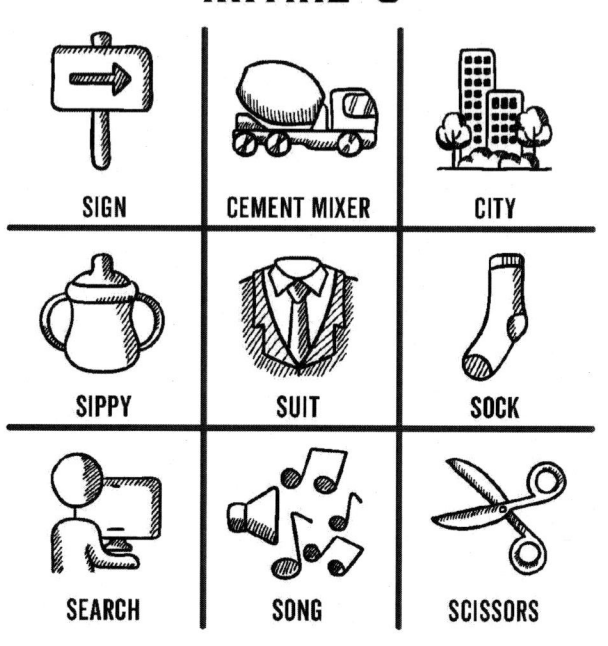

SIGN	CEMENT MIXER	CITY
SIPPY	SUIT	SOCK
SEARCH	SONG	SCISSORS

MEDIAL S

ICE CREAM	CASSETTE	POPSICLE
UNICYCLE	BASEBALL	BICYCLE
DRESSER	CROSSWALK	PASTA

FINAL S

FENCE	BALANCE	HOUSE
POLICE	COMPASS	ICE
HORSE	MOOSE	DRESS

ALL RIGHTS RESERVED © 2017 PEACHIESPEECHIE.COM

I CAN SAY THE S SOUND!

Listen to the words on the left as they are read aloud. Then, draw a line to match the word to the corresponding picture on the right side of the page. Then, practice saying the word with an accurate S sound.

MATCHING INITIAL S

SOCK

SAIL

CITY

SUIT

SANDAL

SING

I CAN SAY THE S SOUND!

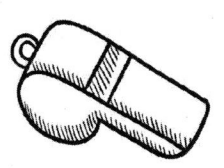

Listen to the words on the left as they are read aloud. Then, draw a line to match the word to the corresponding picture on the right side of the page. Then, practice saying the word with an accurate S sound.

MATCHING MEDIAL S

ERASER

MESSY

DRESSER

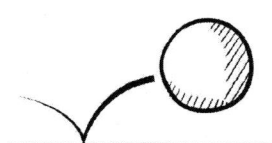

BICYCLE

WHISTLE

BOUNCING

ALL RIGHTS RESERVED © 2017 peachiespeechie.com

I CAN SAY THE S SOUND!

Listen to the words on the left as they are read aloud. Then, draw a line to match the word to the corresponding picture on the right side of the page. Then, practice saying the word with an accurate S sound.

MATCHING FINAL S

HOUSE

DICE

BUS

DANCE

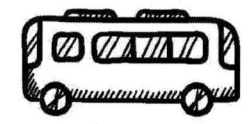

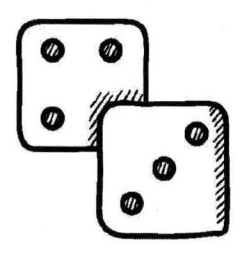

RACE

PASS

ALL RIGHTS RESERVED © 2017 peachiespeechie.com

S CLUES: CUT AND PASTE

Cut out the pictures at the bottom of the page. Read the clues and then select the picture that the clues are describing. Glue the picture in the corresponding box and then practice the S word 10 times.

S CLUES INITIAL S

I am slippery. You can find me in a bathroom. I help clean your hands and body. What am I? →

I am very small. You plant me in the ground. With water and soil, I can grow into a big plant. What am I? →

I am a hot ball of gasses burning far away. I light up the Earth. I am bright and yellow. What am I? →

I am soft. You can wear me on your feet. I keep your toes warm. What am I? →

ALL RIGHTS RESERVED © 2016 PEACHIESPEECHIE.COM

| Sun |  Sock |  Soap |  Seed | 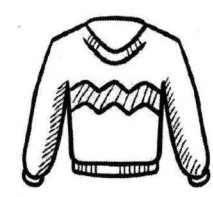 Sweater |

S CLUES: CUT AND PASTE

Cut out the pictures at the bottom of the page. Read the clues and then select the picture that the clues are describing. Glue the picture in the corresponding box and then practice the S word 10 times.

S CLUES INITIAL S

I'm a cute animal. I live in cold areas. I am a good swimmer and I eat fish. What am I? →

I'm made from balls of snow. Put a scarf around my neck and a hat on my head and I'll decorate your yard. What am I? →

Slip me on your feet on a hot summer day. Your toes are free to wiggle while you walk around outside. What am I? →

I'm sharp and made of metal. I can cut paper into shapes. I can give you a haircut, too! What am I? →

ALL RIGHTS RESERVED © 2016 PEACHIESPEECHIE.COM

| Soccer Ball | Scissors | Snowman | Sandals | Seal |

S CLUES: CUT AND PASTE

Cut out the pictures at the bottom of the page. Read the clues and then select the picture that the clues are describing. Glue the picture in the corresponding box and then practice the S word 10 times.

S CLUES MEDIAL S

I'm something you can eat. I'm warm and covered in sauce. I'm slippery and squishy. What am I? →

I'm something you tell other people. You can say it or write it down. I give people information. What am I? →

I'm fast and I make a rumbling sound. I have two wheels and an engine too. What am I? →

I'm a marked off area on the pavement where you can cross the street. What am I? →

ALL RIGHTS RESERVED © 2016 PEACHIESPEECHIE.COM

| Pasta | 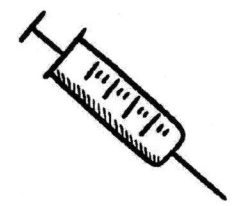 Vaccine |  Message |  Crosswalk |  Motorcycle |

75

S CLUES: CUT AND PASTE

Cut out the pictures at the bottom of the page. Read the clues and then select the picture that the clues are describing. Glue the picture in the corresponding box and then practice the S word 10 times.

S CLUES MEDIAL S

I'm a large creature that lived a very long time ago. I am extinct now. I have pointy claws and sharp teeth. What am I? →

I'm small and made of metal or plastic. When you blow air through me, I make a loud sound. What am I? →

I'm a curved flakey bread. I am golden brown and delicious. I am often eaten for breakfast. What am I? →

I'm icy cold and come in many flavors. I'm a sweet treat, but I may melt on a hot sunny day. What am I? →

ALL RIGHTS RESERVED © 2016 PEACHIESPEECHIE.COM

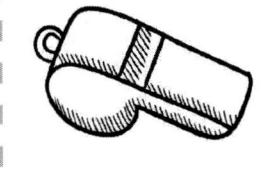

| Insect | Popsicle | Whistle | Croissant | Dinosaur |

S CLUES: CUT AND PASTE

S CLUES FINAL S

Cut out the pictures at the bottom of the page. Read the clues and then select the picture that the clues are describing. Glue the picture in the corresponding box and then practice the S word 10 times.

I'm a building people live in. I have bedrooms, bathrooms, and a kitchen. What am I? →

I'm a set of small white cubes with dots on each surface. I'm often used during board games. What am I? →

I'm a sport. When you play, you hit a small yellow ball back and forth across a court with a racket. What am I? →

I'm a large vehicle. People buy tickets to ride on me. I can take you short distances around the city or all the way across the country. →

ALL RIGHTS RESERVED © 2016 PEACHIESPEECHIE.COM

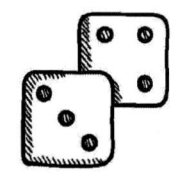

| House | Chess | Bus | Dice | Tennis |

S CLUES: CUT AND PASTE

Cut out the pictures at the bottom of the page. Read the clues and then select the picture that the clues are describing. Glue the picture in the corresponding box and then practice the S word 10 times.

S CLUES FINAL S

I'm a round tool that tells you the direction you are traveling. I always point North. I'm handy when hiking. What am I? →

I'm a sturdy material used for building houses and other buildings. Stack me high to make a wall. What am I? →

I'm planks of wood around a yard. I may also have a gate. I'm tall and often seen on farms to keep animals in one spot. What am I? →

I'm sparkly and pretty. I am a piece of jewelry you wear around your neck. What am I? →

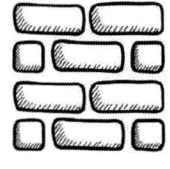

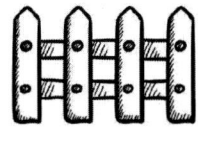

ALL RIGHTS RESERVED © 2016 PEACHIESPEECHIE.COM

| Bricks | Compass | Purse | Necklace | Fence |

SILLY S SENTENCES: READ AND ILLUSTRATE

INITIAL S

Say the sentences below using your best S sound. Then, illustrate the silly scene in the space provided.

Sally stole two salads from her sister's table.

Steve wore his scuba suit to the city mall.

The cymbals Stephanie bought were on sale.

SILLY S SENTENCES: READ AND ILLUSTRATE

INITIAL S

Say the sentences below using your best S sound. Then, illustrate the silly scene in the space provided.

He stirred the soup on the stove with a sword.

Seven soft kittens slept in seven silly socks.

On Saturday the surfers ate sausages on the beach.

SILLY S SENTENCES: READ AND ILLUSTRATE

INITIAL S

Say the sentences below using your best S sound. Then, illustrate the silly scene in the space provided.

Several striped bees stung Samantha on Sunday.

The sign said to sing before crossing the street.

Stan the seal saw six fish dancing in the sea.

ALL RIGHTS RESERVED © 2017 PEACHIESPEECHIE.COM

SILLY S SENTENCES: READ AND ILLUSTRATE

MEDIAL S

Say the sentences below using your best S sound. Then, illustrate the silly scene in the space provided.

Bossy Bessy has very messy hair.

I keep my dinosaur fossils beside my bicycle.

Kelsey the dancer danced with a baseball.

SILLY S SENTENCES: READ AND ILLUSTRATE

MEDIAL S

Say the sentences below using your best S sound. Then, illustrate the silly scene in the space provided.

Hester has a collection of racing insects.

Missy put erasers in her popsicles.

The grasshopper has huge muscles.

SILLY S SENTENCES: READ AND ILLUSTRATE

FINAL S

Say the sentences below using your best S sound. Then, illustrate the silly scene in the space provided.

Bess the Moose likes to eat purple grass.

The horse carried lettuce in his purse.

On the bus, Tess spilled juice on her dress.

SILLY S SENTENCES: READ AND ILLUSTRATE

FINAL S

Say the sentences below using your best S sound. Then, illustrate the silly scene in the space provided.

When it's hot, Horace melts ice on his face.

Yes, I jumped the fence to escape the mutant mouse.

It's not nice to erase your teacher's notes from the board.

STORY TIME
INITIAL S

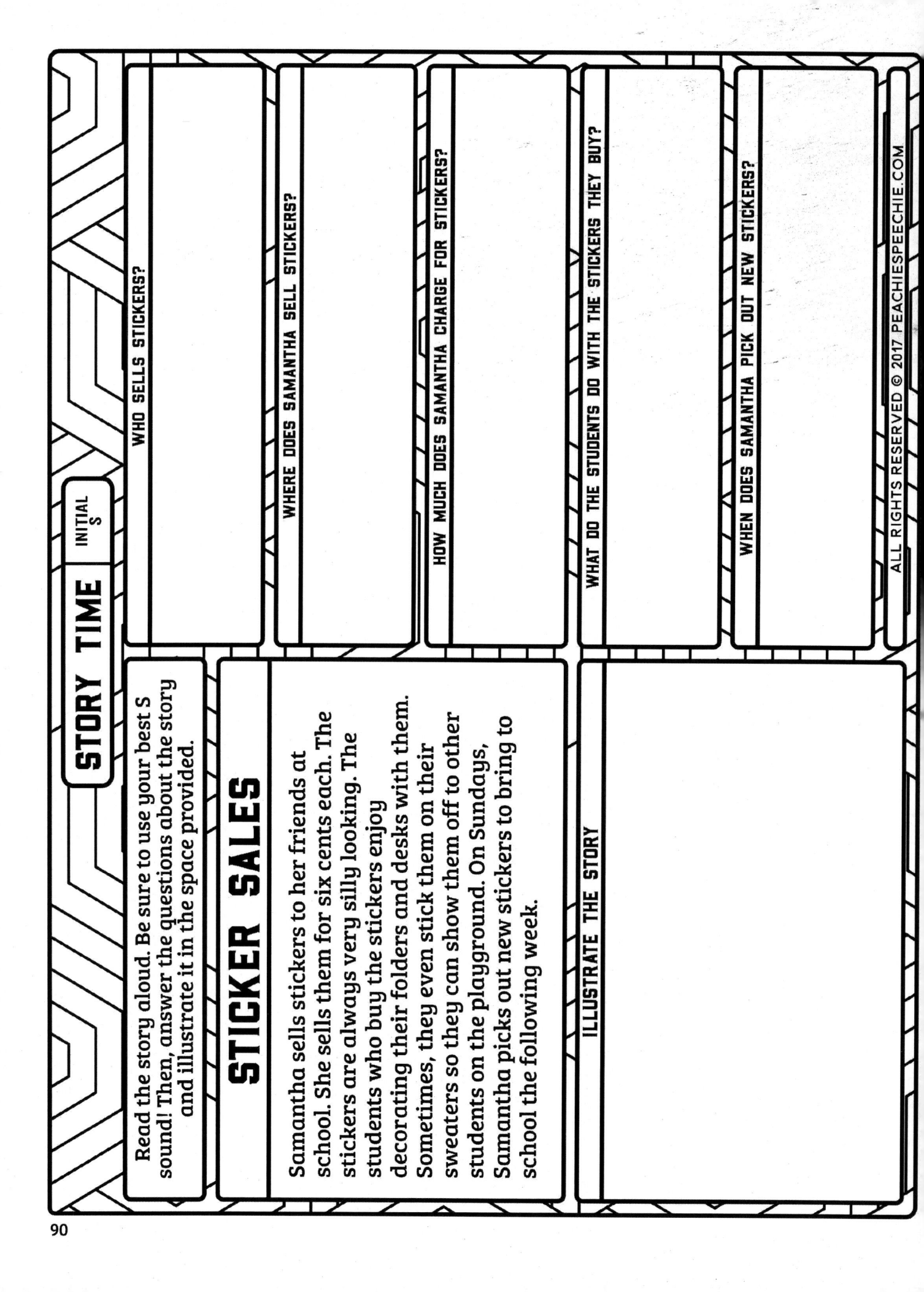

Read the story aloud. Be sure to use your best S sound! Then, answer the questions about the story and illustrate it in the space provided.

STICKER SALES

Samantha sells stickers to her friends at school. She sells them for six cents each. The stickers are always very silly looking. The students who buy the stickers enjoy decorating their folders and desks with them. Sometimes, they even stick them on their sweaters so they can show them off to other students on the playground. On Sundays, Samantha picks out new stickers to bring to school the following week.

WHO SELLS STICKERS?

WHERE DOES SAMANTHA SELL STICKERS?

HOW MUCH DOES SAMANTHA CHARGE FOR STICKERS?

WHAT DO THE STUDENTS DO WITH THE STICKERS THEY BUY?

WHEN DOES SAMANTHA PICK OUT NEW STICKERS?

ILLUSTRATE THE STORY

ALL RIGHTS RESERVED © 2017 PEACHIESPEECHIE.COM

STORY TIME — INITIAL S

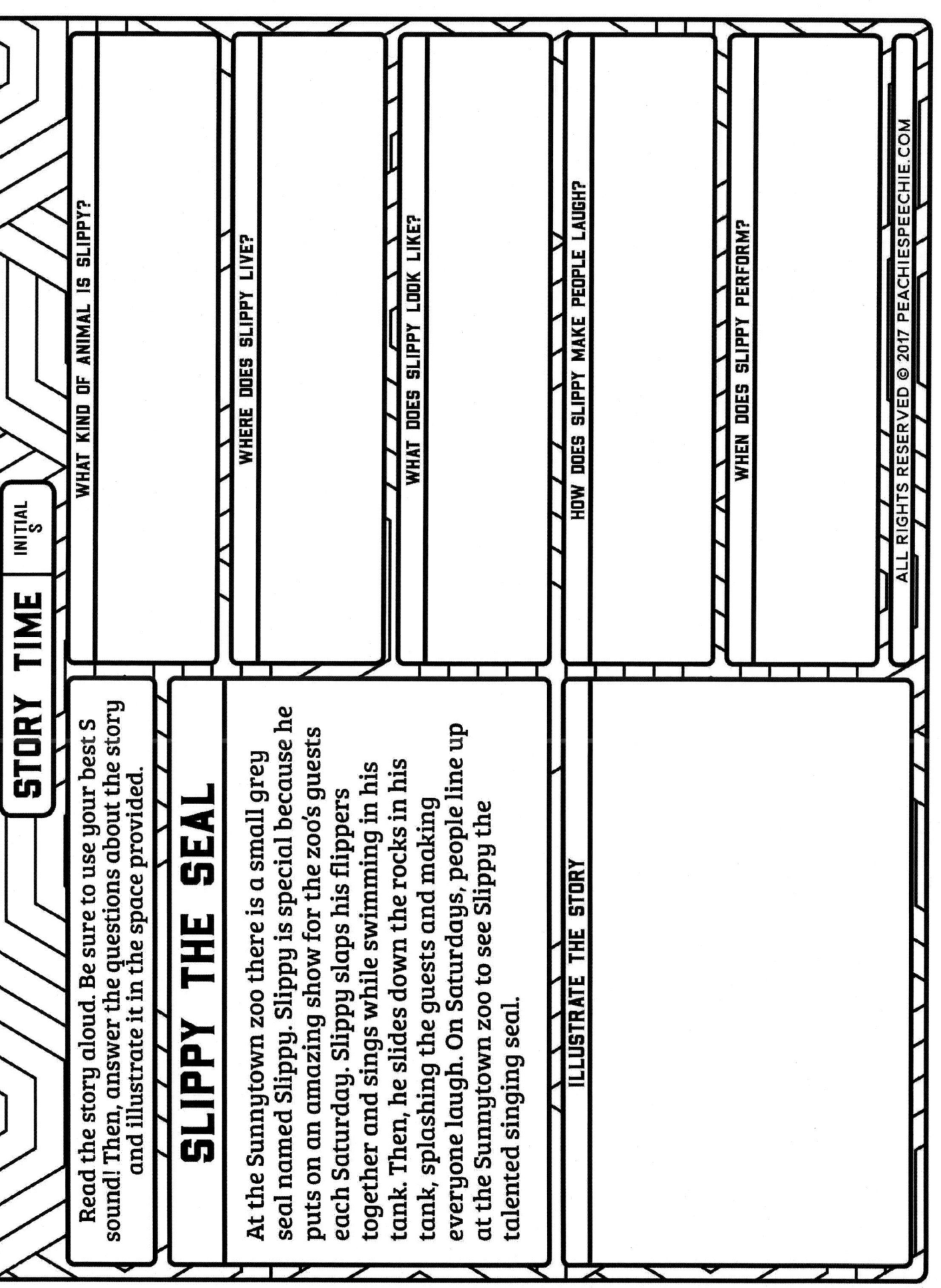

Read the story aloud. Be sure to use your best S sound! Then, answer the questions about the story and illustrate it in the space provided.

SLIPPY THE SEAL

At the Sunnytown zoo there is a small grey seal named Slippy. Slippy is special because he puts on an amazing show for the zoo's guests each Saturday. Slippy slaps his flippers together and sings while swimming in his tank. Then, he slides down the rocks in his tank, splashing the guests and making everyone laugh. On Saturdays, people line up at the Sunnytown zoo to see Slippy the talented singing seal.

WHAT KIND OF ANIMAL IS SLIPPY?

WHERE DOES SLIPPY LIVE?

WHAT DOES SLIPPY LOOK LIKE?

HOW DOES SLIPPY MAKE PEOPLE LAUGH?

WHEN DOES SLIPPY PERFORM?

ILLUSTRATE THE STORY

ALL RIGHTS RESERVED © 2017 PEACHIESPEECHIE.COM

STORY TIME — INITIAL S

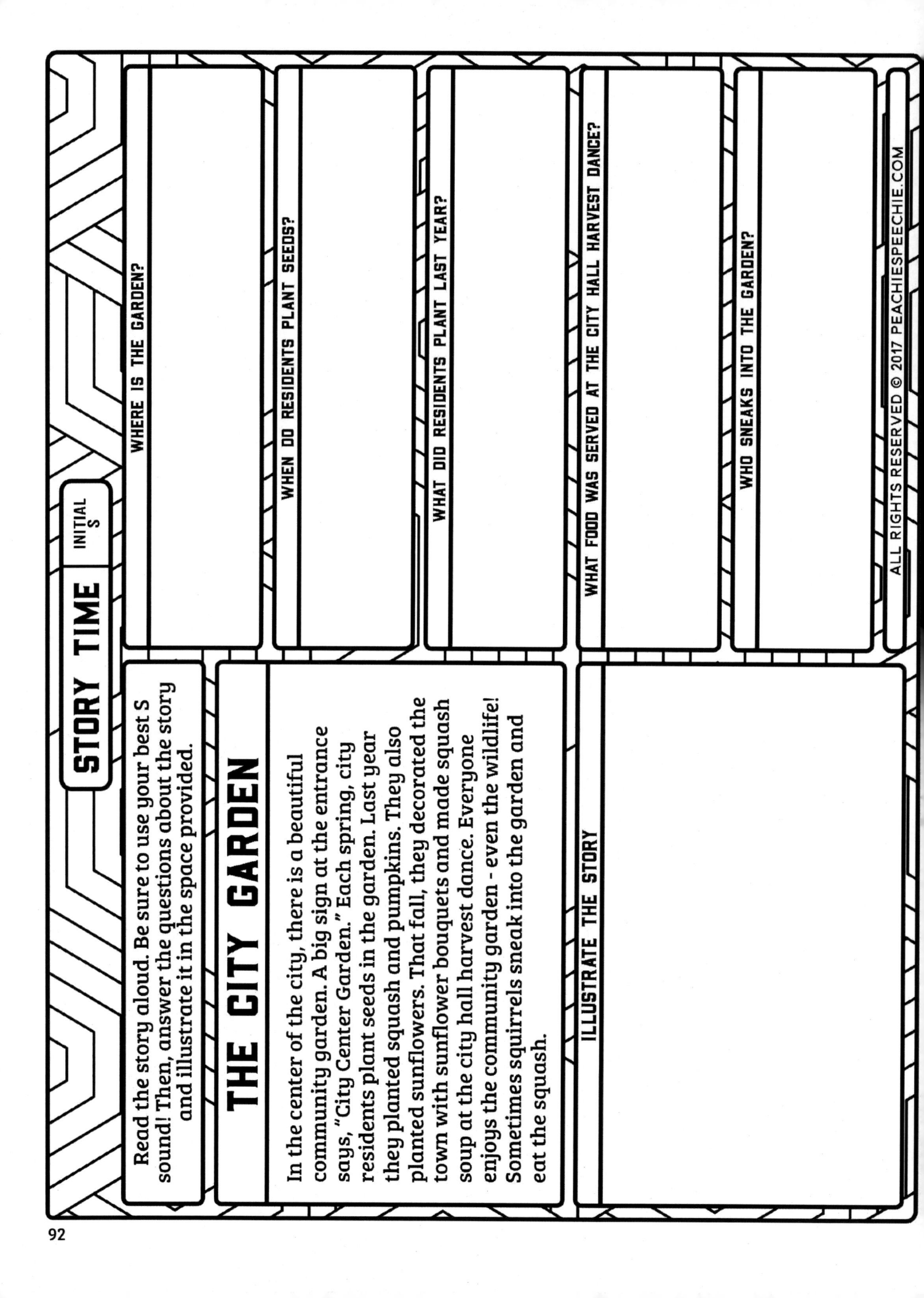

Read the story aloud. Be sure to use your best S sound! Then, answer the questions about the story and illustrate it in the space provided.

THE CITY GARDEN

In the center of the city, there is a beautiful community garden. A big sign at the entrance says, "City Center Garden." Each spring, city residents plant seeds in the garden. Last year they planted squash and pumpkins. They also planted sunflowers. That fall, they decorated the town with sunflower bouquets and made squash soup at the city hall harvest dance. Everyone enjoys the community garden - even the wildlife! Sometimes squirrels sneak into the garden and eat the squash.

WHERE IS THE GARDEN?

WHEN DO RESIDENTS PLANT SEEDS?

WHAT DID RESIDENTS PLANT LAST YEAR?

WHAT FOOD WAS SERVED AT THE CITY HALL HARVEST DANCE?

WHO SNEAKS INTO THE GARDEN?

ILLUSTRATE THE STORY

ALL RIGHTS RESERVED © 2017 PEACHIESPEECHIE.COM

STORY TIME — INITIAL S

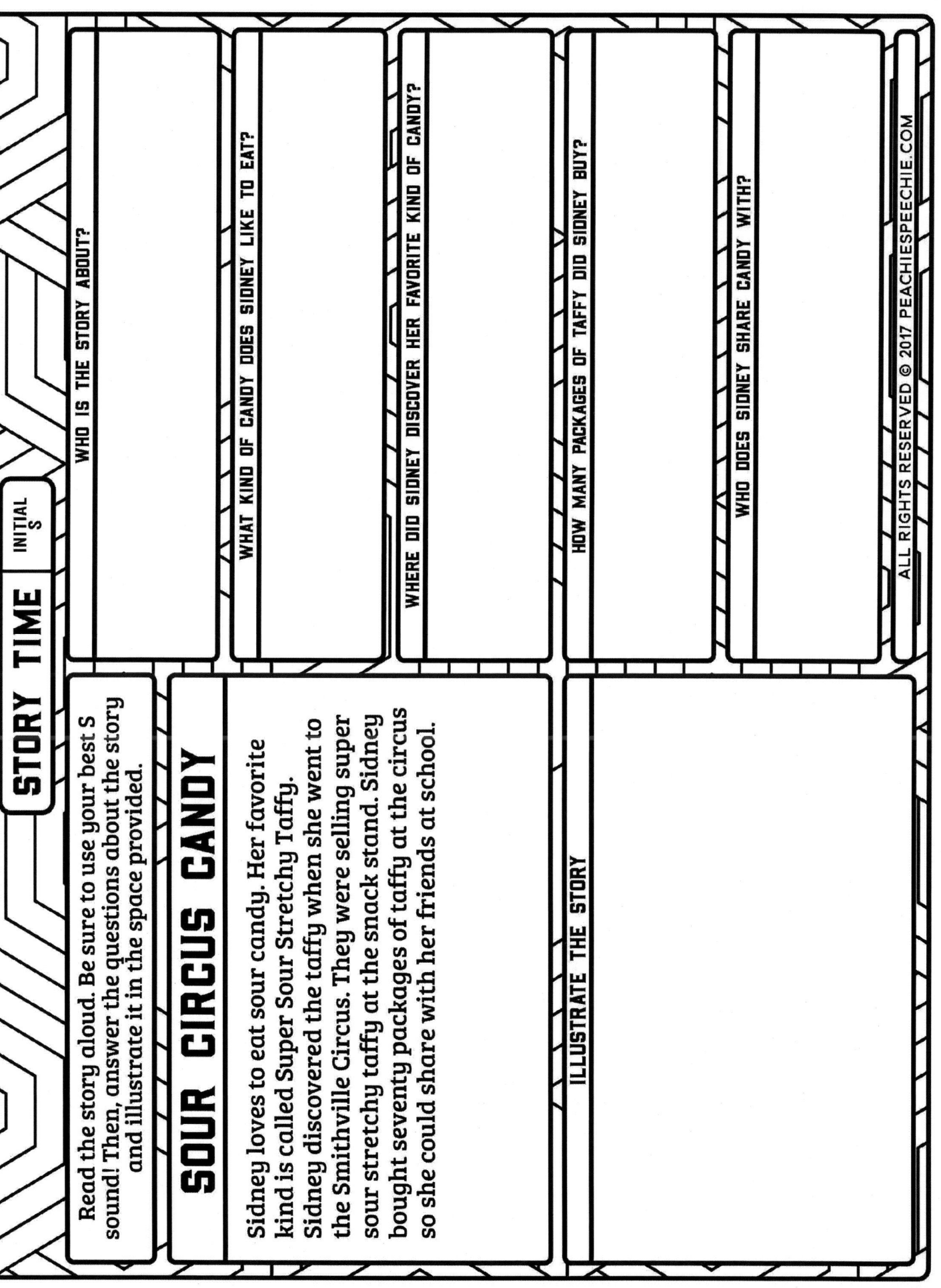

Read the story aloud. Be sure to use your best S sound! Then, answer the questions about the story and illustrate it in the space provided.

SOUR CIRCUS CANDY

Sidney loves to eat sour candy. Her favorite kind is called Super Sour Stretchy Taffy. Sidney discovered the taffy when she went to the Smithville Circus. They were selling super sour stretchy taffy at the snack stand. Sidney bought seventy packages of taffy at the circus so she could share with her friends at school.

WHO IS THE STORY ABOUT?

WHAT KIND OF CANDY DOES SIDNEY LIKE TO EAT?

WHERE DID SIDNEY DISCOVER HER FAVORITE KIND OF CANDY?

HOW MANY PACKAGES OF TAFFY DID SIDNEY BUY?

WHO DOES SIDNEY SHARE CANDY WITH?

ILLUSTRATE THE STORY

ALL RIGHTS RESERVED © 2017 PEACHIESPEECHIE.COM

STORY TIME

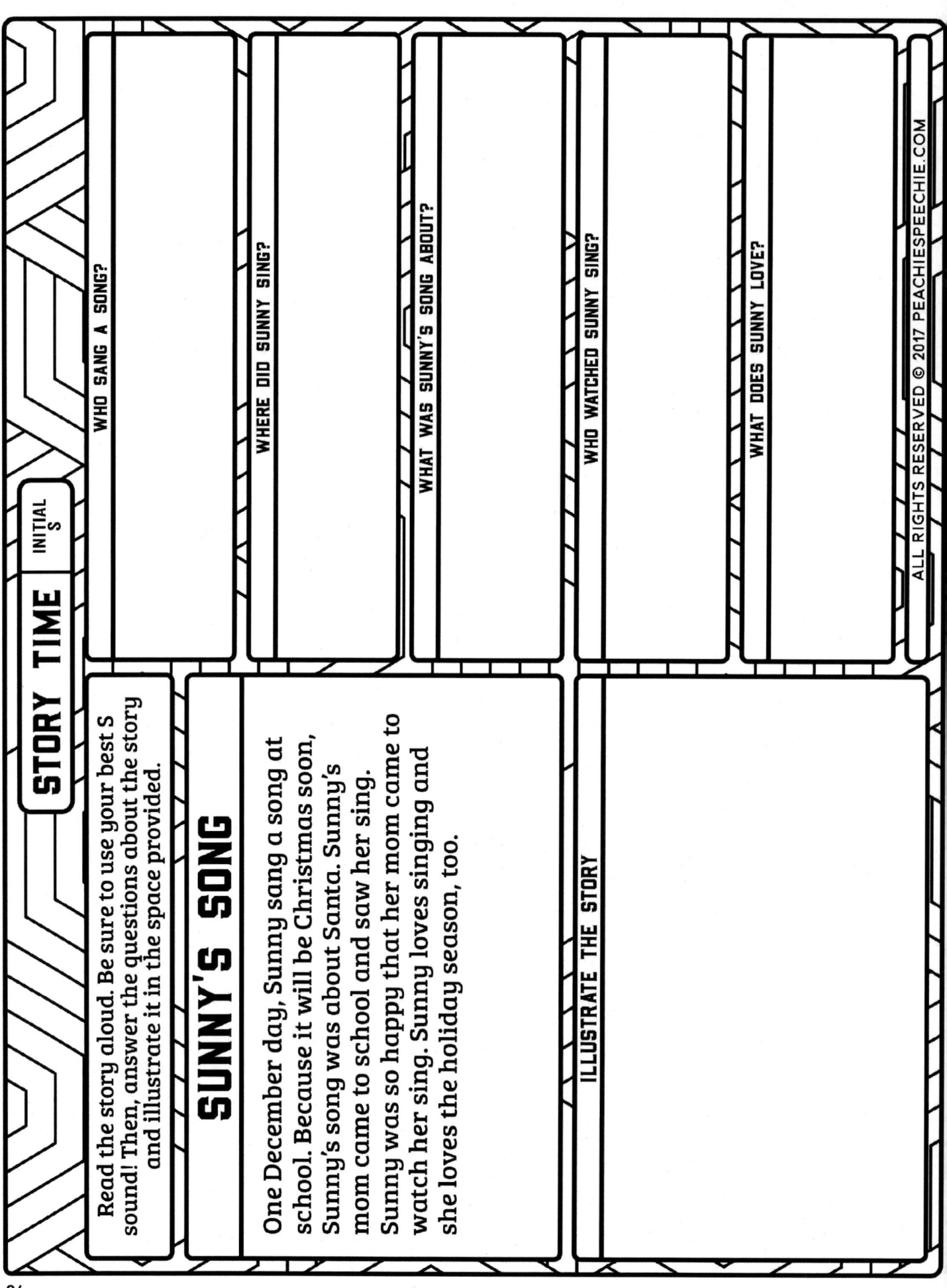

INITIALS

Read the story aloud. Be sure to use your best S sound! Then, answer the questions about the story and illustrate it in the space provided.

SUNNY'S SONG

One December day, Sunny sang a song at school. Because it will be Christmas soon, Sunny's song was about Santa. Sunny's mom came to school and saw her sing. Sunny was so happy that her mom came to watch her sing. Sunny loves singing and she loves the holiday season, too.

WHO SANG A SONG?

WHERE DID SUNNY SING?

WHAT WAS SUNNY'S SONG ABOUT?

WHO WATCHED SUNNY SING?

WHAT DOES SUNNY LOVE?

ILLUSTRATE THE STORY

ALL RIGHTS RESERVED © 2017 PEACHIESPEECHIE.COM

STORY TIME — MEDIAL S

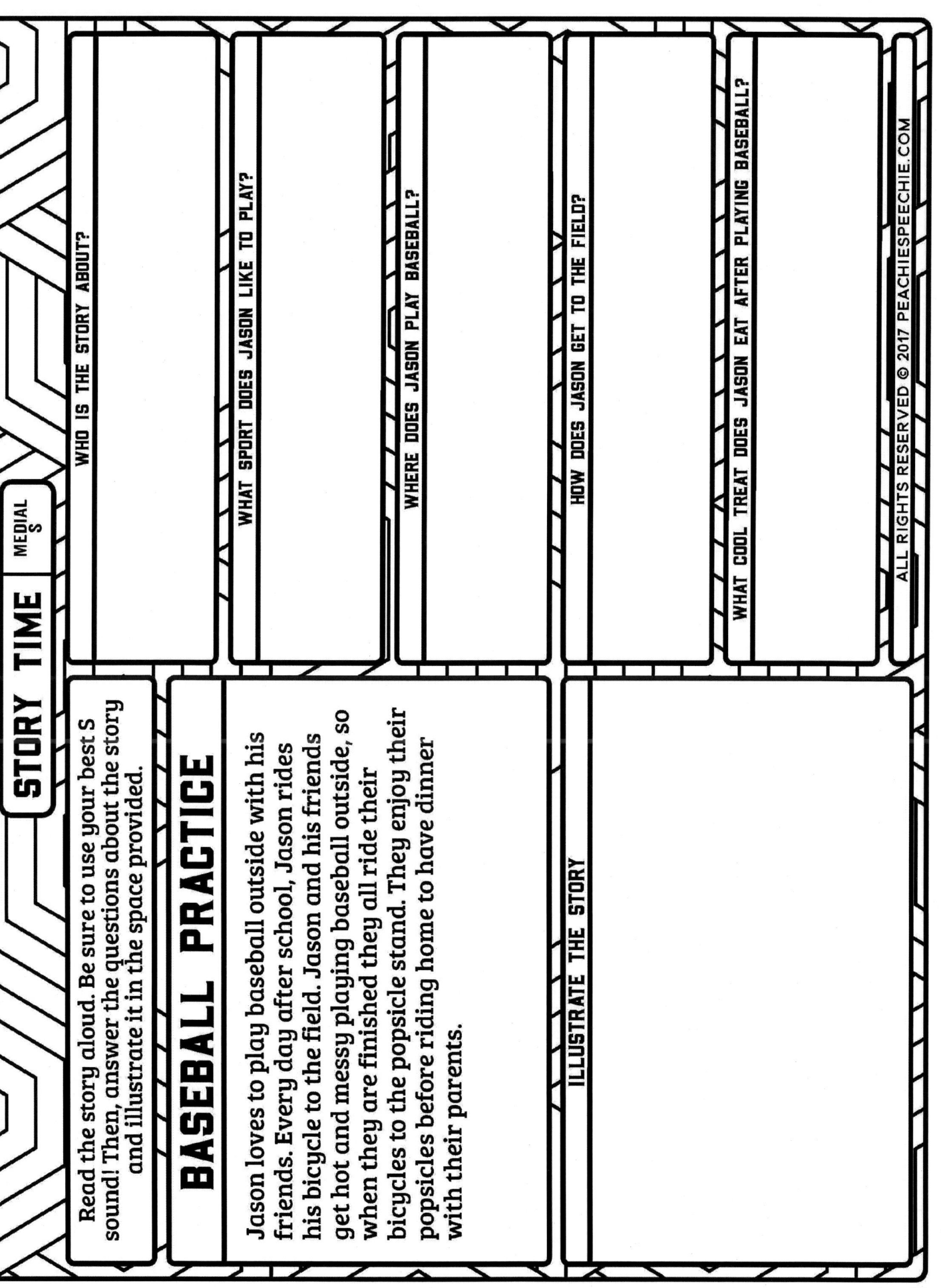

Read the story aloud. Be sure to use your best S sound! Then, answer the questions about the story and illustrate it in the space provided.

BASEBALL PRACTICE

Jason loves to play baseball outside with his friends. Every day after school, Jason rides his bicycle to the field. Jason and his friends get hot and messy playing baseball outside, so when they are finished they all ride their bicycles to the popsicle stand. They enjoy their popsicles before riding home to have dinner with their parents.

WHO IS THE STORY ABOUT?

WHAT SPORT DOES JASON LIKE TO PLAY?

WHERE DOES JASON PLAY BASEBALL?

HOW DOES JASON GET TO THE FIELD?

WHAT COOL TREAT DOES JASON EAT AFTER PLAYING BASEBALL?

ILLUSTRATE THE STORY

ALL RIGHTS RESERVED © 2017 PEACHIESPEECHIE.COM

STORY TIME
MEDIAL S

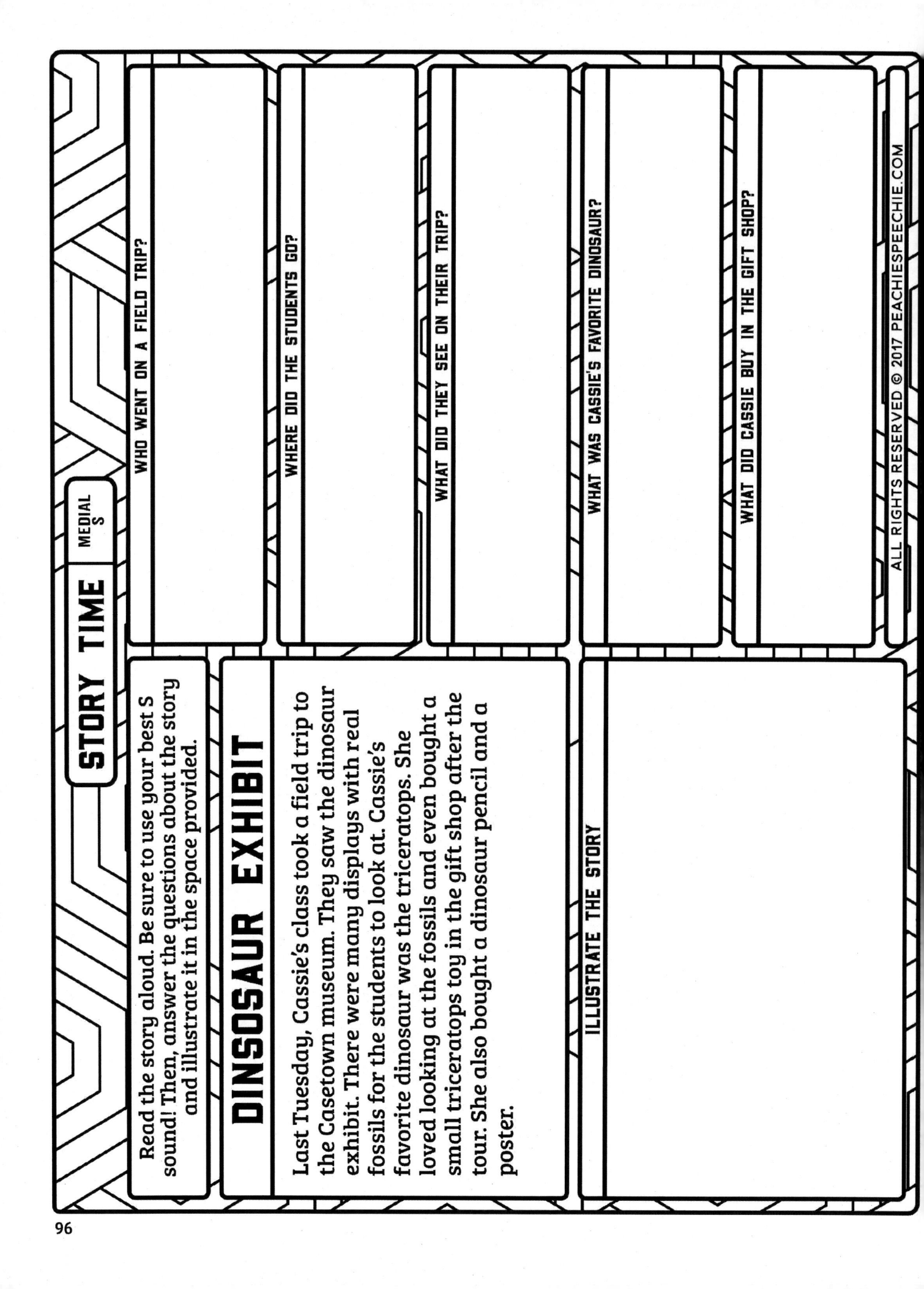

Read the story aloud. Be sure to use your best S sound! Then, answer the questions about the story and illustrate it in the space provided.

DINOSAUR EXHIBIT

Last Tuesday, Cassie's class took a field trip to the Casetown museum. They saw the dinosaur exhibit. There were many displays with real fossils for the students to look at. Cassie's favorite dinosaur was the triceratops. She loved looking at the fossils and even bought a small triceratops toy in the gift shop after the tour. She also bought a dinosaur pencil and a poster.

WHO WENT ON A FIELD TRIP?

WHERE DID THE STUDENTS GO?

WHAT DID THEY SEE ON THEIR TRIP?

WHAT WAS CASSIE'S FAVORITE DINOSAUR?

WHAT DID CASSIE BUY IN THE GIFT SHOP?

ILLUSTRATE THE STORY

ALL RIGHTS RESERVED © 2017 PEACHIESPEECHIE.COM

STORY TIME
MEDIAL S

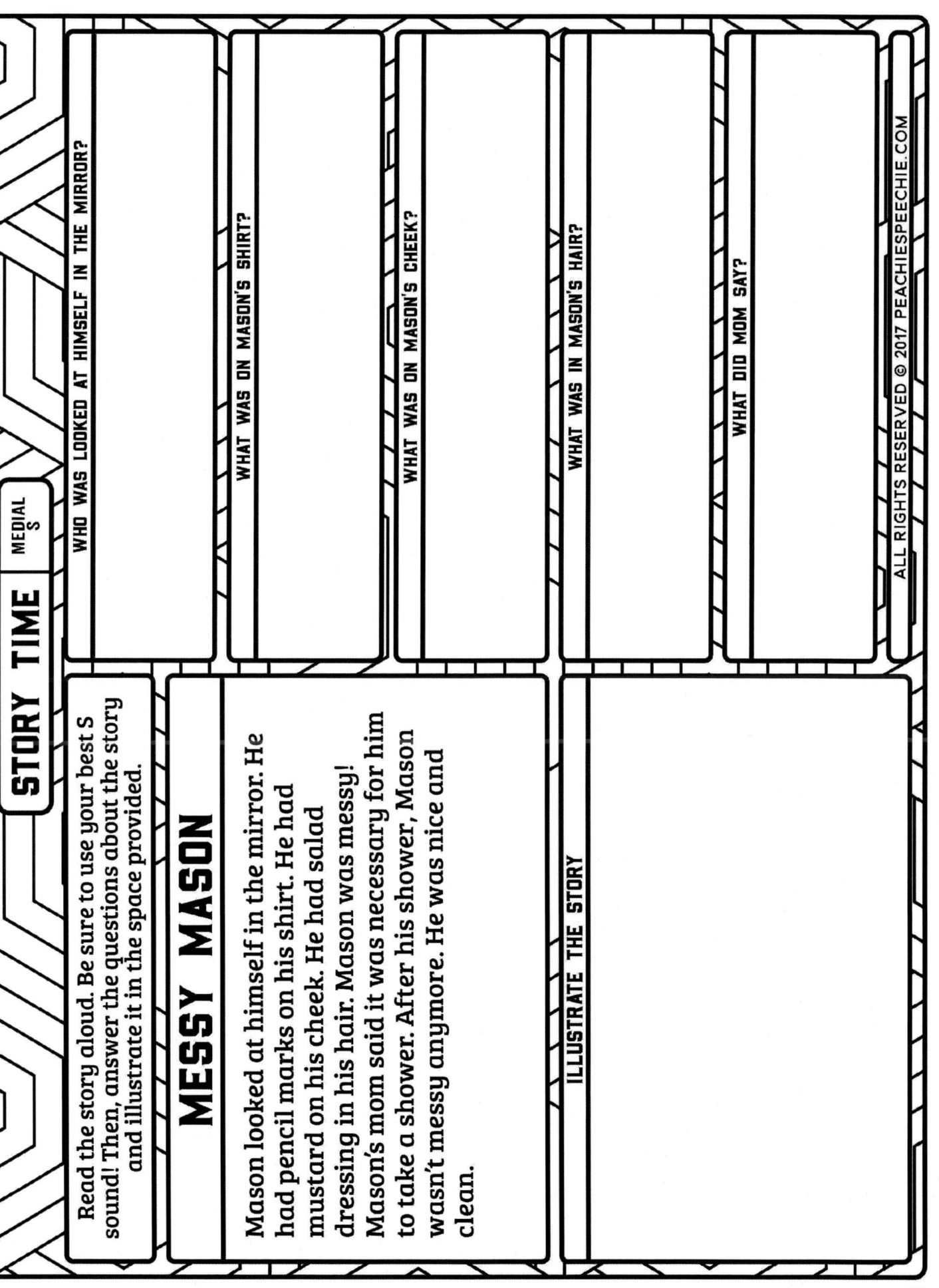

Read the story aloud. Be sure to use your best S sound! Then, answer the questions about the story and illustrate it in the space provided.

MESSY MASON

Mason looked at himself in the mirror. He had pencil marks on his shirt. He had mustard on his cheek. He had salad dressing in his hair. Mason was messy! Mason's mom said it was necessary for him to take a shower. After his shower, Mason wasn't messy anymore. He was nice and clean.

WHO WAS LOOKED AT HIMSELF IN THE MIRROR?

WHAT WAS ON MASON'S SHIRT?

WHAT WAS ON MASON'S CHEEK?

WHAT WAS IN MASON'S HAIR?

WHAT DID MOM SAY?

ILLUSTRATE THE STORY

ALL RIGHTS RESERVED © 2017 PEACHIESPEECHIE.COM

STORY TIME — MEDIAL S

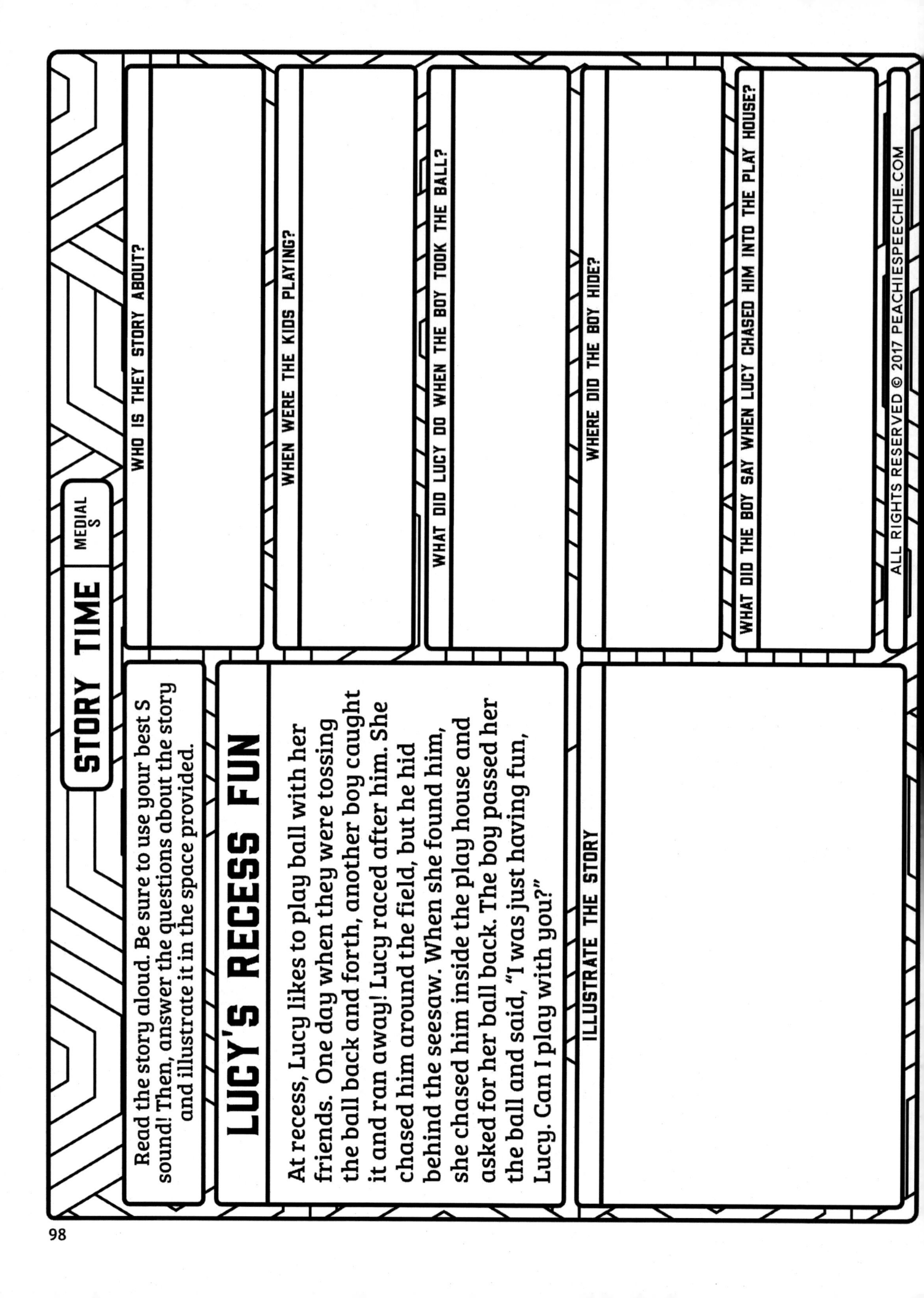

Read the story aloud. Be sure to use your best S sound! Then, answer the questions about the story and illustrate it in the space provided.

LUCY'S RECESS FUN

At recess, Lucy likes to play ball with her friends. One day when they were tossing the ball back and forth, another boy caught it and ran away! Lucy raced after him. She chased him around the field, but he hid behind the seesaw. When she found him, she chased him inside the play house and asked for her ball back. The boy passed her the ball and said, "I was just having fun, Lucy. Can I play with you?"

WHO IS THEY STORY ABOUT?

WHEN WERE THE KIDS PLAYING?

WHAT DID LUCY DO WHEN THE BOY TOOK THE BALL?

WHERE DID THE BOY HIDE?

WHAT DID THE BOY SAY WHEN LUCY CHASED HIM INTO THE PLAY HOUSE?

ILLUSTRATE THE STORY

ALL RIGHTS RESERVED © 2017 PEACHIESPEECHIE.COM

STORY TIME

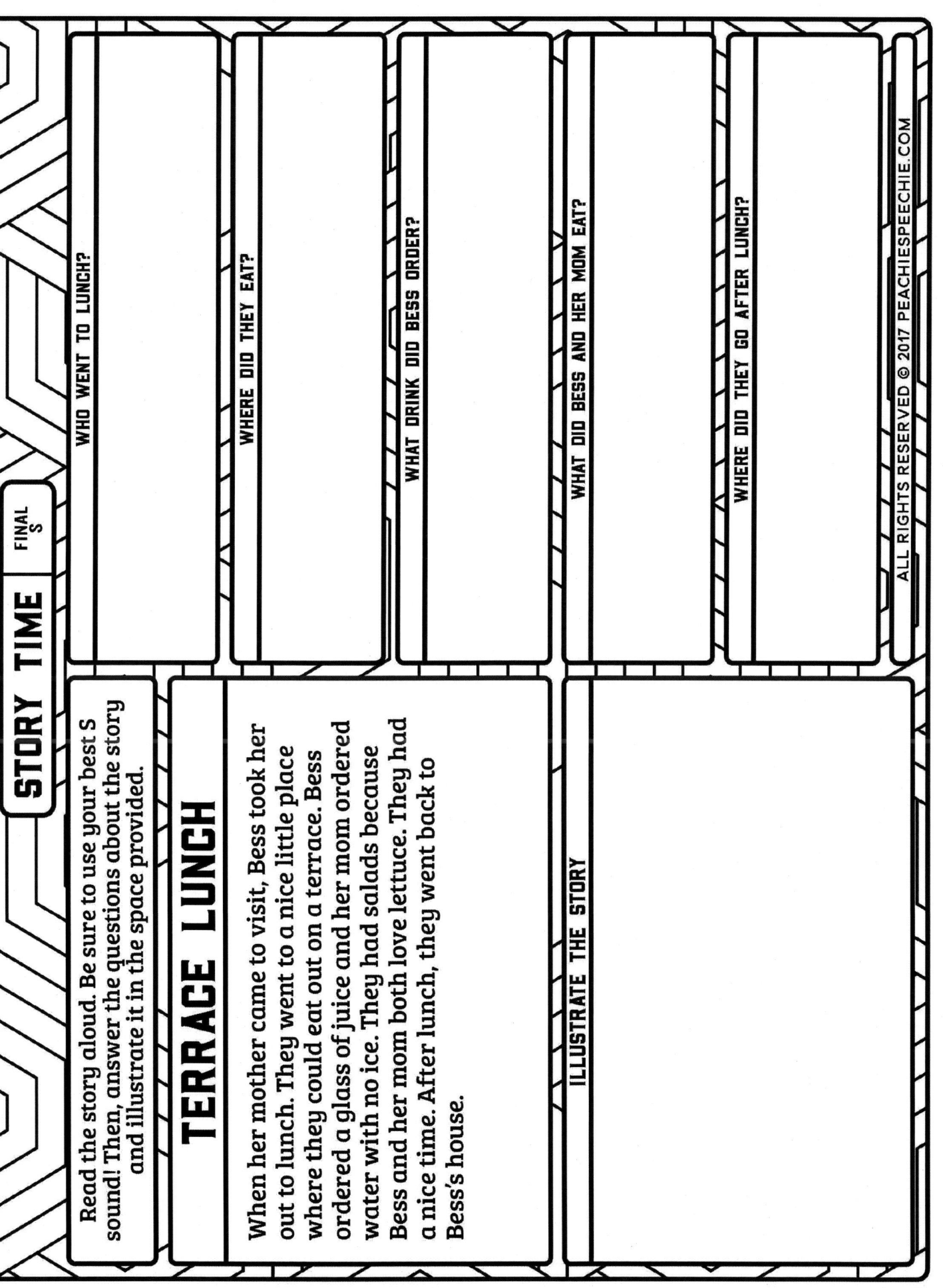

FINAL S

Read the story aloud. Be sure to use your best S sound! Then, answer the questions about the story and illustrate it in the space provided.

TERRACE LUNCH

When her mother came to visit, Bess took her out to lunch. They went to a nice little place where they could eat out on a terrace. Bess ordered a glass of juice and her mom ordered water with no ice. They had salads because Bess and her mom both love lettuce. They had a nice time. After lunch, they went back to Bess's house.

WHO WENT TO LUNCH?

WHERE DID THEY EAT?

WHAT DRINK DID BESS ORDER?

WHAT DID BESS AND HER MOM EAT?

WHERE DID THEY GO AFTER LUNCH?

ILLUSTRATE THE STORY

ALL RIGHTS RESERVED © 2017 PEACHIESPEECHIE.COM

STORY TIME — FINAL S

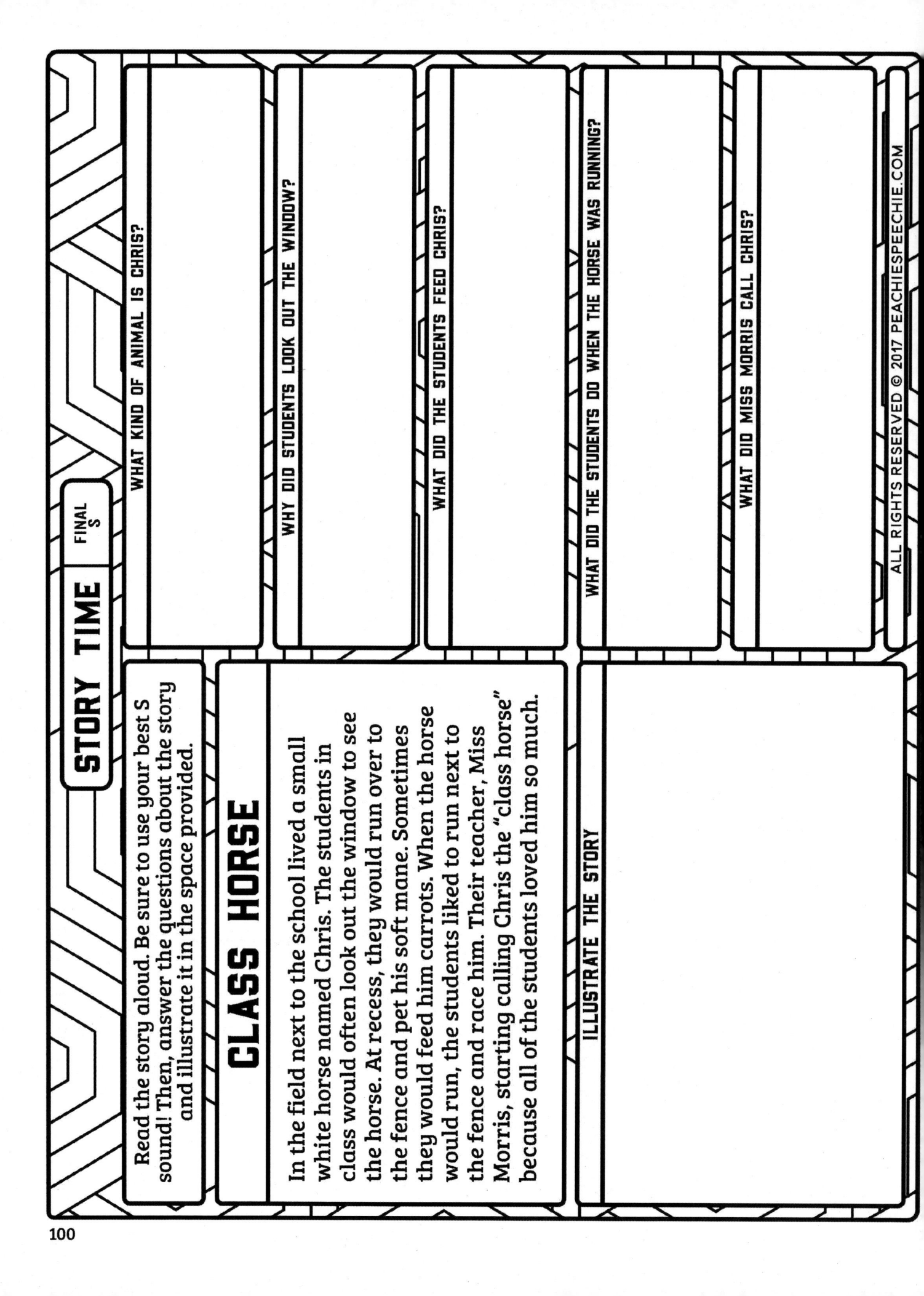

Read the story aloud. Be sure to use your best S sound! Then, answer the questions about the story and illustrate it in the space provided.

CLASS HORSE

In the field next to the school lived a small white horse named Chris. The students in class would often look out the window to see the horse. At recess, they would run over to the fence and pet his soft mane. Sometimes they would feed him carrots. When the horse would run, the students liked to run next to the fence and race him. Their teacher, Miss Morris, starting calling Chris the "class horse" because all of the students loved him so much.

WHAT KIND OF ANIMAL IS CHRIS?

WHY DID STUDENTS LOOK OUT THE WINDOW?

WHAT DID THE STUDENTS FEED CHRIS?

WHAT DID THE STUDENTS DO WHEN THE HORSE WAS RUNNING?

WHAT DID MISS MORRIS CALL CHRIS?

ILLUSTRATE THE STORY

ALL RIGHTS RESERVED © 2017 PEACHIESPEECHIE.COM

STORY TIME

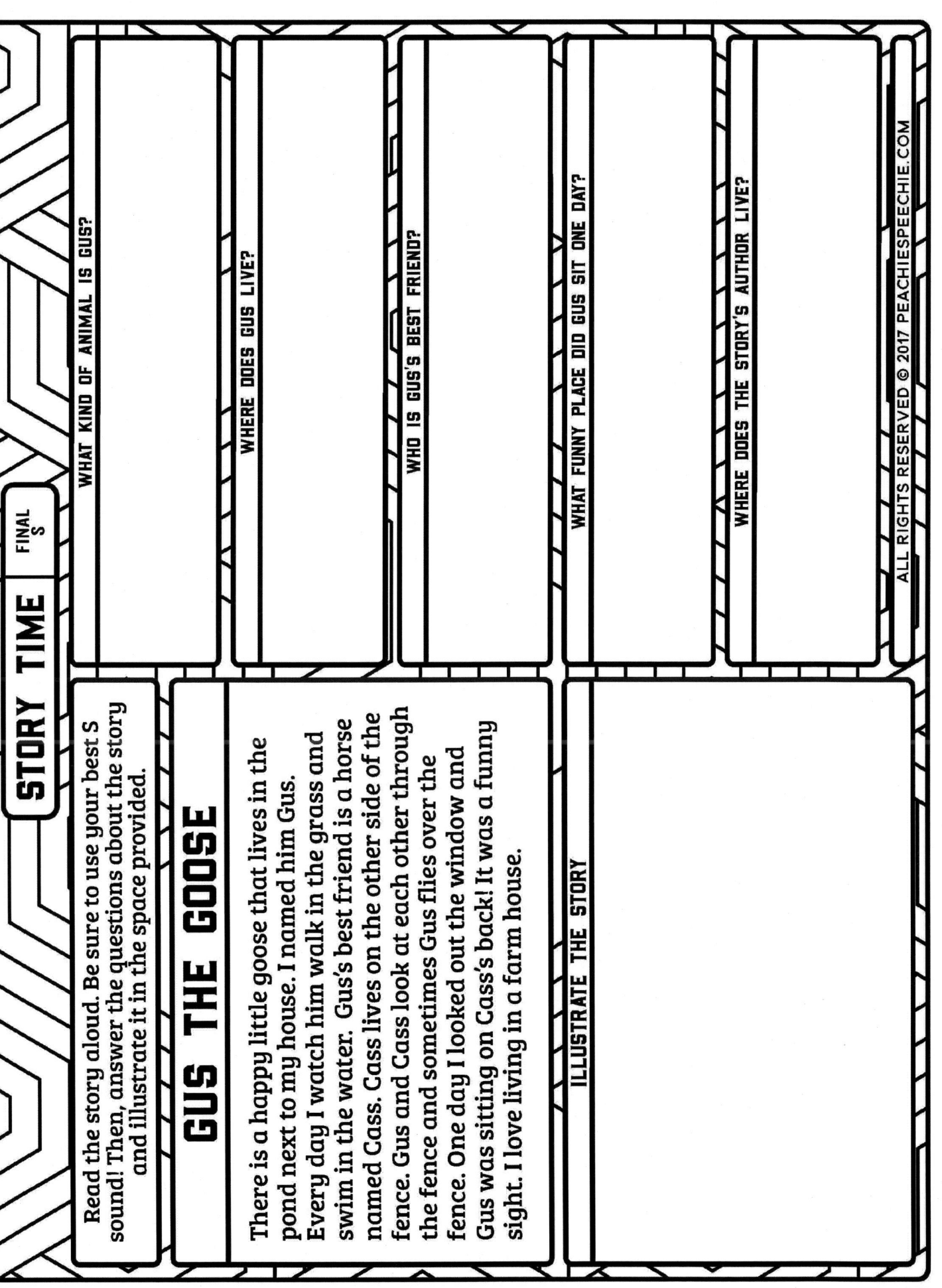

FINAL S

Read the story aloud. Be sure to use your best S sound! Then, answer the questions about the story and illustrate it in the space provided.

GUS THE GOOSE

There is a happy little goose that lives in the pond next to my house. I named him Gus. Every day I watch him walk in the grass and swim in the water. Gus's best friend is a horse named Cass. Cass lives on the other side of the fence. Gus and Cass look at each other through the fence and sometimes Gus flies over the fence. One day I looked out the window and Gus was sitting on Cass's back! It was a funny sight. I love living in a farm house.

WHAT KIND OF ANIMAL IS GUS?

WHERE DOES GUS LIVE?

WHO IS GUS'S BEST FRIEND?

WHAT FUNNY PLACE DID GUS SIT ONE DAY?

WHERE DOES THE STORY'S AUTHOR LIVE?

ILLUSTRATE THE STORY

ALL RIGHTS RESERVED © 2017 PEACHIESPEECHIE.COM

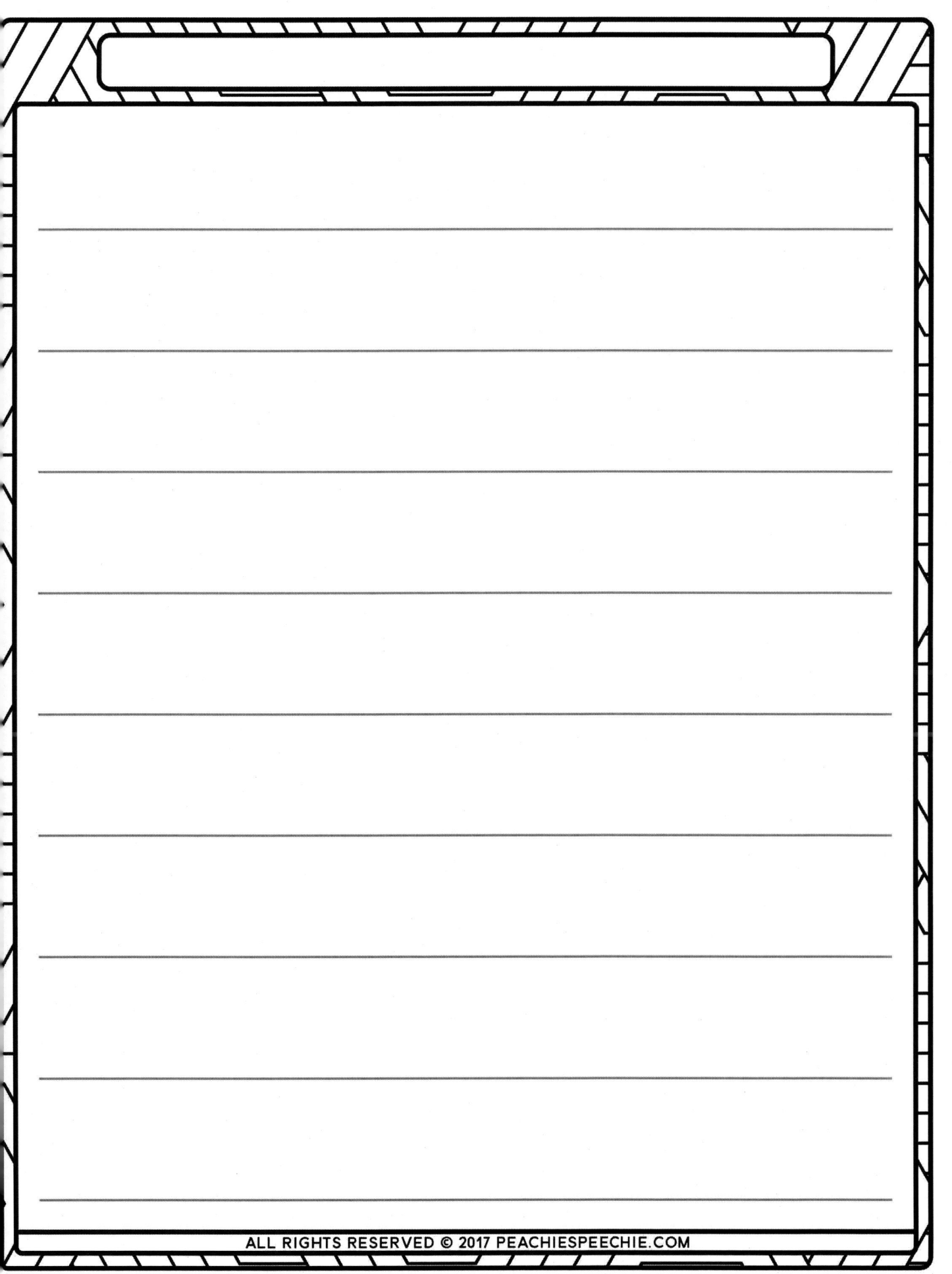

RESOURCES

Berthnal, J., Bankston, N., Flipsen P. (2009). *Articulation and Phonological Disorders: Speech Sound Disorders in Children.* (6th ed.) Boston, MA: Pearson Education, Inc.

Marshalla, P. (2007). *Frontal Lisp Lateral Lisp.* Mill Creek, WA: Marshalla Speech and Language.

Secord, W. (2007). *Eliciting Sounds: Techniques for Clinicians.* (2nd ed.). Clifton Park, NY: Thomson Delmar Learning.

VanRiper, C., Erickson, R. (1996). Speech Correction: An Introduction to Speech Pathology and Audiology. (9th ed.) Needham Heights, MA: Allyn and Bacon.

Made in United States
North Haven, CT
24 October 2022